Trauma and Blessings

Autobiography of a Prussian Immigrant

Henning K. Sehmsdorf

Printed by Applied Digital Imaging, Inc, Bellingham, WA

Life can only be understood backwards; but it must be lived forwards.
(The Journals of Søren Kierkegaard, 1844)

Your vision will become clear only when you can look into your own heart.
Who looks outside, dreams; who looks inside, awakes.
(Letters of Carl Gustav Jung, 1973)

It didn't start with you:
Inherited family trauma shapes who we are.
(Mark Wolynn, 2016)

Table of Contents

Foreword: You Can Take the Boy Out of Prussia,
But Can You Take Prussia Out of the Man? - 1

Homeland: A Brief History of Prussia & Its Virtues - 5

Mother's Family—Rathenow, Braunsberg, Danzig, Thorn, and Wehlau - 23

Father's Family—Sehmsdorf, Dauer, Züsedom, Podanin, Berlin,
Kolmar, Stallupönen, and After - 33

Life of an Immigrant - 61

The Immigrant Paradox — Trauma & Blessings - 95

Sources - 121

Foreword : You can Take the Boy Out of Prussia, But Can You Take Prussia Out of the Man?

Elizabeth, my wife, an inveterate teacher, once said to me that the purpose of education was to overcome the past. What she meant was that as a child she unwittingly adopted certain racist attitudes of her parents and her community in rural Oregon. It took education and self-reflection to raise these prejudices into consciousness and thereby excise them. For her, the past was something to be overcome. As a modern American, she felt that individuation, the gradual process of becoming adult, meant freeing oneself of the constraints of family history and ethnic background — her mother's proud lineage back to the ancestor's disembarking from the ship "Elizabeth" on the shores of New England in the early 1600s, her paternal grandfather's arriving on an unknown vessel from Holland sometime in the late 1800s — and reach for selfhood shaped by personal choice and discovery of her own, unique identity. As a result, she does not know much about her family beyond that of her mother's parents, and even less about her father's, and practically nothing of the many cousins and their families descended from her father's siblings.

For me, by contrast, the past holds the key to who I am, which is why I am writing this book at the end of my life. As an immigrant who in 1956 arrived as a nineteen-year old, looking for educational opportunities denied to me in post-war Germany, the history of my homeland, my mother tongue (and its embedded humor), the grandparents, parents, brothers and sisters I left behind, the social customs, foods, music, and culture — embodied my own past which I had to renegotiate in my new country in a long and painful process of assimilation. Having lived through WWII as a child, I was keenly aware of the ghosts of Germany's Nazi past, of its reputed authoritarian (Prussian) mentality, and of the assumed rigidity of German custom in family life, education, and public discourse. It is not easy for any immigrant to have doors slammed in your face because of your national, ethnic background.

Nonetheless, that background, especially the family's past, have always been a source of pride, comfort, and orientation for me. It mattered to find out that the earliest known ancestor on my father's side was a blacksmith who emigrated to the wilderness of the Prussian provinces on the southern coast of the Baltic to clear the ancient forests and turn the swamps into rich granaries. Probably during the Thirty Years' War (1618-1648), a war that devastated Germany in the bitter struggle between the Protestant North led by Sweden and the Catholic South led by Bavaria, this smith left his village in Schleswig-Holstein (now the northernmost state of Germany bordering on Denmark), adopting its name as his family's own. His son became a smallholder farmer in Prussia, and his grandson (my great-great-grandfather) became a major landowner who purchased a 4,000-acre manor farm from a baron impoverished by military service to the royal court in Berlin. The acquisition of the manor by a commoner was remarkable because at the time non-nobles were rarely allowed to hold land of that size, and the purchase had to be specifically sanctioned by the Crown. From then on the family lived in the spirit of nobility, expressed in my father's favorite slogan, *noblesse oblige* (nobility carries obligation), which meant that a people had to act honorably in carrying out their social responsibilities.

It also mattered to discover that on my mother's side the earliest traceable ancestors were fisherfolk on the Baltic Sea, tanners and other craftsmen and women, and that in one sudden generation they rose above their social station to become physicians, factory owners, and one of them president of the Prussian parliament. My mother's father, a physician, an intelligent and kindly man, became a huge presence in my childhood, largely replacing my own father who was absent, fighting the war for six long years.

This book gives a biographical account of my own past and that of my family, both before I emigrated to the United States, and since then. In telling my story, I want to recall experiences and memories that have shaped my life and continue to do so in the present. Some of these experiences are remembered as traumatic, others as blessings. In talking to my brothers and

sisters as an adult, I have been struck by how differently we remember many events in the past, making me realize that the living past is as much an imagined dream as it is a distillation of historical fact. But either way it represents lived, and therefore true, experience. In understanding the past, I have come to understand myself.

The book is organized into five chapters. The first chapter looks at the development of the Duchy of Brandenburg into the powerhouse of Prussia, which eventually became the largest state in Germany under the leadership of the absolute Hohenzollern monarchy. The chapter examines how the rise of Prussia squared with the so-called Prussian virtues identified with the Christian ethos of the Teutonic Knights and raised to a principle of governance by the Calvinist monarchs. These principles evolved into commonly shared behavioral and culture codes, all the way to the contemporary German standards of efficiency, austerity and discipline. The chapter, however, also shows the fundamental contradiction between the patriotism of individual self-sacrifice and the systemic violence inherent in an empire built on expansion of state power and territory at the expense of foreign populations. The most egregious example of this contradiction was found in the step-by-step dismemberment of the Kingdom of Poland and the Grand Duchy of Lithuania, and the violent suppression of non-German ethnicities, their culture and language, in the tragic arc of expansionist empire building and its aftermath.

The second and third chapters delineate the history of the family on my Mother's and my Father's sides, evolving from craftspeople and peasants into urban and landed elites (*Großbürger*). The chapters show the role of progressive educational reforms in the 18th century to provide needed leadership in state administration, the military, church, sciences, and arts, and the progressive liberation of peasants from the shackles of serfdom, resulting in a new balance of power between the landed nobility and rural workers. Also shown is how the paternalism of the monarchical state is mirrored in the culture of the Prussian family, particularly in the authority of the father. As modeled by the monarch, the authority of parents to instill the Prussian virtues could be effective only when embedded in patience, kindness and tolerance.

The fourth chapter tells the story of my own emigration from Germany to find a new home in America, working in a meat factory in Indiana and attending community college, serving in the U.S. Army in Missouri, studying philosophy of science at the University of Rochester, and earning a doctorate at the University of Chicago, followed by teaching at the University of Washington and establishing a family of my own, while also building a biodynamic farm on Lopez Island.

The fifth chapter weighs the balance of my experience in the light of recent socio-cultural studies of the challenges faced by immigrants, and their children, of living between two worlds, the old one they left behind and the new one they chose. My children faced the challenge of living in America with a father who holds a world view, primary language, and values that differ from the mainstream culture the children had to fit into. The success or failure of the relationship between immigrants and their children, depends on how well they negotiate conflicting world views and behavioral codes.

Homeland: A Brief History of Prussia and Its Virtues

Old Prussia

The Kingdom of Prussia — which until after WWI constituted the largest state in Germany — took its name from a region at the south-eastern shore of the Baltic Sea between the Weichsel River (Polish Vistula) to the west, and the Kurische Nehrung (Curonian Sound) — a freshwater lagoon formed nearly ten millennia ago — to the east.

Slavic stock. The tribal names were toponymic, derived from native terms for the thousands of lakes, streams, swamps, and wetlands dotting the coastal region, which provided natural barriers against intrusion from outside. Archeologists documented continuous occupation of the area from the Iron Age (500 BC) to early conquests by Slavic groups pushing north and west during the Migration Period, which started with the invasion of Europe by Asian Huns about 375 AD,

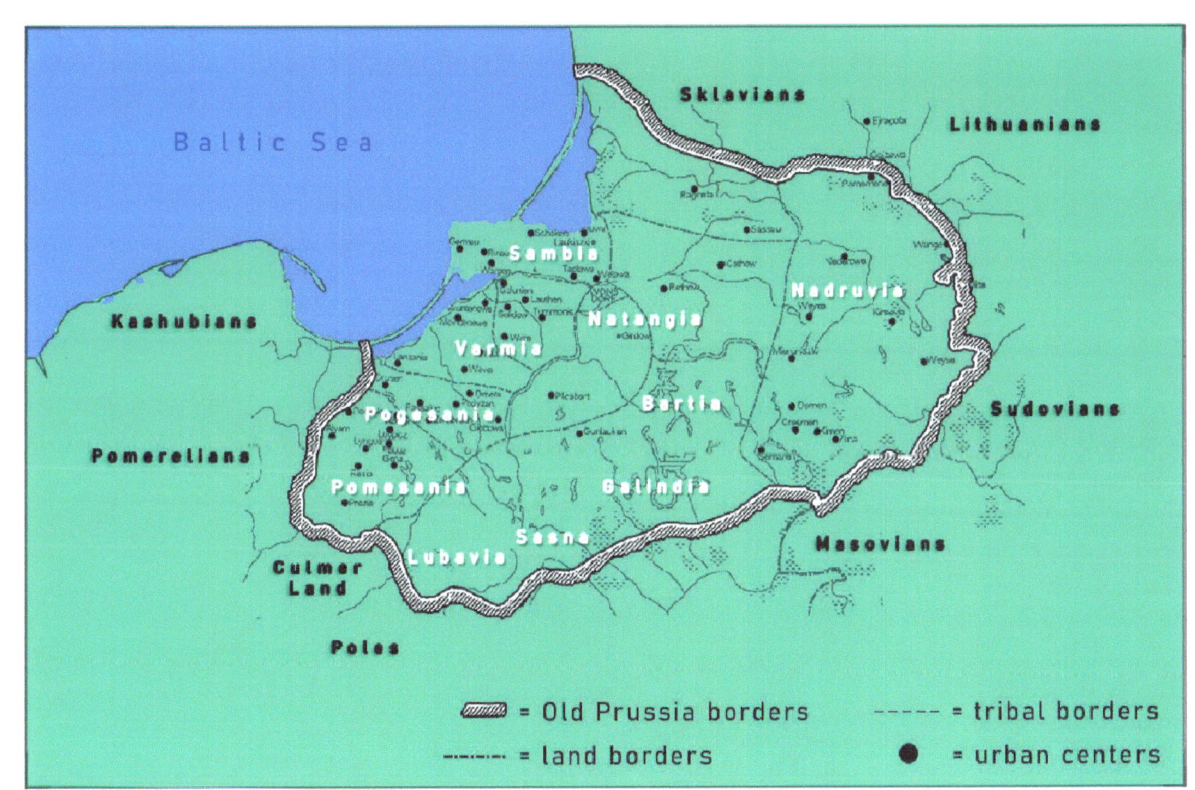

Old Prussian independent tribes 12th century

The region was originally inhabited by tribes known as Borussi (German *Pruzzen* or Old Prussians), an indigenous people of Baltic-

and with the collapse of the Western Roman Empire. The Old Prussians spoke an Indo-European language and practiced polytheistic animism and ancestor worship. In their world view all of nature was sacred and alive both with helpful and demonic spirits. According to Baltic mythology, the Kurische Nehrung was formed by a giantess playing on the seashore. The name of the Kuren Spit is tied to the Coronians, a subgroup of Old Prussians. The population lived on fishing and small farming in family settlements separated from neighboring farmsteads by forest, swamp and marsh. Households were headed by the *buttataws* (from *buttan* meaning "home" and *taws*, meaning "father").

For safety, adjacent farms formed a *laūks* ("field") around a hill fort. Community authority rested in the adult males, who elected the chief (*rikīs*) in charge of border defense, watch towers, and roads. Groups of *laūks* formed tribal units of up to two thousand people and covered up to a hundred-and-twenty square miles. However, the *lauks* never fused into a political organization or state, which weakened Old Prussia in the face of intrusion from abroad.

From the eighth to the early eleventh centuries, the Kuren Spit was the location of Kaup (from Old Norse meaning "purchase"), a major Viking trade center and likely starting point of the ancient Amber Road connecting the Baltic Sea to the Mediterranean. Kaup is also the name of a hill immediately north, where a large burial site with Swedish grave goods, swords and arrows, was found. Protected by a garrison, Kaup flourished as a market until the end of the tenth century, when Danes repeatedly raided the coast. The Spit may have been the home of the last living speaker of the Old Prussian language, which disappeared in the seventeenth century. Some elements of traditional Kuren cuisine, for example *Kurenkaffee*, vodka flavored

Marienburg Castle built in 13th century

with coffee and honey, remained popular in East Prussia in modern times. Kaup, today called Mokhovoye, is now part of the Kaliningrad Oblast, an exclave of Russia.

The Teutonic Knights

In the thirteenth century, Old Prussia was occupied by the Teutonic Order, a military religious order founded in 1190-1191 by German knights taking monastic vows of poverty, chastity and obedience during the Third Crusade. After the fall of Acre (near Jerusalem) to the Moslems, the order dedicated itself to the Christianization of Eastern Europe. Answering a call by Polish Duke Conrad of Masovia, the Teutonic Knights initiated a crusade against the Old Prussians and subdued them after fifty years of struggle. They built their castles on top of Old Prussian fortifications at Memel (1252, today Klaipėda, Lithuania), Neuhausen (1283, today Guryevsk, Russia), and Rositten (1372, today Rybachy, Russia).

The Old Prussians, who repeatedly rose in rebellion against the Knights, were reduced to serfdom, and German settlers brought in from the West took ownership of the land. Cisterian monks assumed a leading role in draining swamps to make the land usable for agricultural production, and in improving livestock breeding.

Resisting Polish ambitions to expand their territory northward, the Knights put the lands later known as East and West Prussia under papal suzerainty and laid the foundation of the Prussian state centered on Marienburg (today Malbork, Poland), the largest castle in the world.

In 1237, the Teutonic Knights merged with the Livonian Brothers, another German religious order that conquered the pagan populations of modern-day Lithuania, Latvia and Estonia. By 1472, the

Knights and the Brothers held most of the territories south of the Baltic Sea.

Brandenburg-Prussia

With the Protestant Reformation of the early sixteenth century, the governance of the lands colonized by the Teutonic Knights changed

Teutonic Order, 1472

radically. In 1525, Albert, Grandmaster of the Knights, converted to the Lutheran faith, and the Order ceased to exist as a Catholic institution. Instead, Albert became secular hereditary Duke of Prussia under Polish suzerainty. When his male line died out in 1618, Albert's grandson, Georg-Wilhelm, Margrave of Brandenburg (1619-1640), inherited the Prussian duchy and became Duke of Brandenburg-Prussia.

The Margraves of Brandenburg ruled over a population of four-hundred thousand in a marshland of some ten-thousand square miles in the Havel watershed. Originally settled by the Germanic Semnones who were driven out by Slavic Wends, the area was eventually colonized by Saxons who converted the Wends to Christianity in the twelfth century. In 1356 the Margrave was proclaimed Elector of the Holy Roman Empire. In 1415, a Hohenzollern prince from Swabia ascended to the Brandenburg throne. In 1539, the Brandenburg House converted to Lutheranism. Georg-Wilhelm, who had been raised in the Netherlands as a Calvinist, ruled his Lutheran people with tolerance. Mild by temperament, and without a standing army, he found himself buffeted by Protestant and Catholic forces sweeping through Brandenburg during the Thirty Years' War (1618-1648). Over half the

population was killed or dislocated.

The Great Elector

By contrast, the Duke's son, Friedrich-Wilhelm (1620-1688) was a resolute military leader who came to be known as the Great Elector after defeating the Swedes at Fehrbellin (1675). He reorganized the army to lay the foundation of Brandenburg-Prussia as a great European power. In 1668 he introduced the Prussian General Staff which became a model for other European militaries. To fund the army, he developed iron, cotton, linen, lace, wool, soap, and paper industries. He centralized state administration on the mercantilist model, with the interests of the absolute ruler taking precedence over merchants, the nobility, and peasants. He offered tax relief to landowners in compensation for abolishing the feudal Estates (*Landstände)*, the organizations of clergy, nobility, and commoners who traditionally assembled to deliberate legislation and taxation. He improved transportation by connecting rivers with canals that opened Berlin to ocean traffic. A man of learning, he established the Berlin University and Library. To bolster the technical crafts and industry, he strengthened his father's program of settling immigrants in areas depopulated by the War: Protestants (Huguenots) from France, the Netherlands, northern Germany, and Switzerland, and Jews and Catholics from Austria.

The Soldier King

The Elector's policies were continued by his successors, the "Soldier King," Friedrich-Wilhelm I (1688-1740) and the latter's son, Friedrich II, also known as The Great

(1740-1786). Friedrich II famously said: "All religions are equal and good, to the degree that people professing their faith are honest, and even if they are Turks and Pagans, as long as they are willing to populate the land, let them build their mosques and churches as they see fit." His policy of religious tolerance became a defining feature of the realm.

By 1701, Friedrich-Wilhelm succeeded in elevating his status to king, and from then until the dissolution of the Holy Roman Empire at the hands of Napoleon in 1806, the Hohenzollern realms were referred to as **Kingdom of Prussia**, or simply Prussia, whose power became equal to that of Sweden under Charles XI (1660–1697), France under Louis XIV (1643–1715), and Russia under Peter the Great (1682–1725).

Self Portrait, Friedrich-Wilhelm I, 1737

The "Soldier King" greatly increased the infantry's rate of fire by introducing the iron ramrod, but he never started a war. In 1733, he replaced unreliable mercenary forces with a uniquely Prussian system of military service by all male youths as a civic responsibility. The universal draft system stayed in force until the Revolutionary Wars in 1792, when Friedrich Wilhelm II (1786-1797) exempted the sons of the nobility, upperclass commoners, civil servants, and university professors. Universal conscription was re-introduced in 1813 when Prussia declared war against France after Napoleon's invasion of Russia.

A devout Calvinist, the "Soldier King" lived a frugal and austere lifestyle, sold most of his father's personal jewels, furniture, and horses, and in contrast to most other German rulers, left his heir with a sound treasury. In 1732, when twenty thousand Protestants from Catholic Salzburg arrived in Prussia, he personally welcomed and sang Protestant hymns with them. He established schools and hospitals and relieved the middle class of military service in exchange for an annual tax. He cleared forests and drained marshlands to support farming and promoted grain storage to hedge against poor harvests. He personally dictated three hundred pages of Regulations for State Officials describing the responsibilities of every public servant in the realm. Friedrich II described his father as a highly effective ruler: "His spirit was transcendent; he penetrated and understood great objectives, and knew the best interests of his country better than any minister or general." (Mitford 2019, 4). He apparently also possessed remarkable artistic gifts. His self-portrait shows a simply clothed man whose face and body language express physical and inward strength, and a thoughtful demeanor.

However, while the King was a loving and loyal husband, both his wife and his son feared his violent and harsh temper that would flare into cruel physical punishment. The sensitive and intellectual personality of the crown prince enraged the King, who beat the boy when he fell from his horse, or showed preference for reading and playing his flute over military practice or learning statesmanship. In 1730, the seventeen-year old prince tried to flee to his maternal uncle, British King George II, and was put on trial for treason. His twenty-six year old tutor, Count Hans Herman von Katte, one of the king's favorite cavalry officers who taught the prince mathematics and mechanics, and with whom he shared a love of poetry and music, was found guilty of desertion and beheaded in the presence of the boy.

Friedrich was imprisoned at Küstrin Fortress (now Kostrzyn, Poland), stripped of his princely title, and forced to serve as a common foot soldier. In 1733 Friedrich, after long depression, was sufficiently reconciled with his father to be reinstated as Crown Prince, on the condition that he marry his seventeen-year old cousin, Duchess Elisabeth Christine, a relation of the Austrian Hapsburgs.

Friedrich der Große (the Great)

Given military command at the garrison of Ruppin, in 1736 Friedrich and his wife moved to nearby Rheinsberg Castle, where the prince renewed his studies of philosophy, poetry, politics, history and military science. There he began his long correspondence and friendship with the French Enlightenment philosopher Voltaire, with whom he shared an acerbic wit.

Elisabeth produced no children. Historians have speculated that, since Friedrich did not keep mistresses or indulge in sexual affairs the way most rulers of the time did, he must have been homosexual. An alternative argument might be that since Friedrich and Elisabeth were temperamentally and intellectually incompatible, the prince met his need for human warmth and intimacy in the company of intellectual and artistic peers, mostly men, other than his own mother and his older sister, Wilhelmine. It is also possible that the traumatic relationship to his own father left him unsuited for parenthood. How would he have dealt with a recalcitrant heir refusing the destiny to which was born? Emotionally disciplined — some say "cold" — King

The Flute Concert at Sans-Souci by Adolf Menzel, 1852, depicting Frederick playing the flute as C. P. E. Bach accompanies him on a fortepiano.

Among the prince's remarkable works from this period was a treatise on Machiavelli's *The Prince* (1513). Machiavelli had asserted that all successful rulers must embrace evil to assure political survival and growth in power. Friedrich's counter-argument was based on the Enlightenment ideal of benevolent statesmanship for the health and prosperity of the ruler's subjects. The prince squarely aligned himself with his own father's idea of the virtuous ruler as a model for his people. The ruler should be the first servant of the state. Voltaire provided the draft of Friedrich's essay with extensive footnotes and published it as *Anti-Machiavel* in England (Friedrich II, 1740). The loveless political marriage of Friedrich and

Friedrich did not indulge in rages as the Soldier King had to enforce his undeniable sense of justice and duty. Instead, Friedrich poured his seemingly unlimited energies into meeting the responsibilities of his office, and his esthetic sensibilities into music and the visual arts.

Friedrich and Elisabeth treated each other with respect, and he handed her responsibility to represent the crown at the royal court in Berlin. Introverted and uncomfortable with court life, he spent his summers in the intimate setting of his palace at Sans-Souci, the winters in his Potsdam residence, and left it to Elisabeth to receive foreign princes, ambassadors and generals, and entertain the aristocracy and clergy with concerts and public events at court. He admired her charitable work, to which she dedicated more than half of her personal income. When the king died in 1786, at age 74, sitting up in the chair where he had been working to the last, Queen Elisabeth in a letter to his nephew and successor, Friedrich Wilhelm II, praised him as a man who "would have been adored for his great qualities had he been only a private individual; all great princes might take example from him; he reigned like the true father of his people … A true friend himself … he was generous and beneficent, maintained his position without hauteur, and in society was like a private gentleman" (Atkinson, 1958). It seems that the queen understood the complex individuality of the King at a time in when individualism was not an accepted priority, especially for a public person such as a king.

Friedrich II is today remembered as an enlightened absolute monarch who followed his father in modernizing the civil service and judicial system, and allowing non-nobles to become judges and senior bureaucrats. True to his famous statement: "Let everyone seek salvation in his own manner" (*Jeder soll nach seiner eigenen Façon selig werden*), the King pursued a policy of religious tolerance throughout his realm, notwithstanding segregationist protections for Protestant minorities in Silesia after Prussia annexed the province from Catholic Austria. He allowed freedom of the press and literature, and supported the arts, music, theater, writers and philosophers. He preferred French thought over German literature, of which he knew little. Therefore he did not reciprocate the ardent admiration of the greatest German authors of the day, Gotthold Ephraim Lessing (1729–1781) whose plays and critical writings substantially shaped German drama, Johann Wolfgang von Goethe (1749-1832), poet, playwright, novelist, scientist, statesman, theatre director, critic, and author of the immortal *Faust,* and philosopher-poet Friedrich von Schiller (1759-1805).

The King felt on surer ground as a musician and composer of several symphonies, flute concertos, and occasional pieces still performed today. Under the tutelage of Johann Joachim Quantz (1697–1773), flute maker, composer, and flautist highly esteemed by Bach, Hayden and Mozart, Friedrich himself became an excellent flute player and talented composer. Throughout his life, music gave the King respite from the cares and burdens of office. Court music took on greater importance under Friedrich the Great than under any other head of state at the time. His summer

Caravaggio, The Incredulity of Saint Thomas, 1602

palace Sans-Souci was mostly dedicated to the pursuit of his esthetic needs. He invited Johann Sebastian Bach, who composed "Musical Offering" (*Musikalisches Opfer*) for the occasion, a free improvisation of counterpoint fugues on a theme composed by the King (Schmieder, 1950). Bach's sons, Johann Christian and Carl Philipp Emanuel were appointed concert masters at the royal opera, and they accompanied the King during performances at Sans-Souci.

Friedrich did not try his hand at sculpture or painting, as his father had, but surrounded himself with great art works. The exquisite gallery at Sans-Souci, designed by the King himself, held one hundred eighty major works by Caravaggio, Rubens, van Dyke and many other Renaissance and Baroque masters, and ancient and modern French sculpture. The austere exterior of the building displays allegorical sequences of sculpture training and practice, contrasting with the opulent intarsia design of the black and white marble floors inside, white stucco allegories of the arts and science on the ceilings, and well-lit massive displays of gilt-framed paintings on the walls. Here the King would spend hours meditating on the historical and mythological themes of the art works.

In the military and political history of Europe, Friedrich the Great is mostly remembered for battlefield successes and his theoretical contributions to the strategy, tactics, mobility and logistics of warfare. When Friedrich Wilhelm died in 1740, he had left his son an army of about 83,000 out of a population of 2,200,000, a war chest of more than 8,000,000 taler, providing the King with military power that rivaled Russia and France. Like the Soldier King, Friedrich was known as austere and disciplined on and off the battlefield, a reputation well received among his soldiers. Anecdotes of "Old Fred" (*Der Alte Fritz*) prowling an army encampment at night without any insignia on his grey coat and taking a stick to anyone found sleeping at his post, endeared him to his subjects.

Friedrich's brilliant campaigns against Austrian Empress Maria Theresa gained Upper Silesia for Prussia in 1742 and Lower Silesia in 1745. During the Seven Years' War (1756–1763), the temporary alliance of Austria and Russia almost reversed those gains — and the king nearly committed suicide when faced with potential defeat — but Russia's abrupt withdrawal from battle secured victory for the Prussian army and made the annexation of Silesia permanent.

A Russo-Prussian alliance prepared for the three successive partitions of Poland (1772, 1793, 1795), whose territory was absorbed into Prussia to the West, Russia to the East, and Austria to the South. Weakened by internal decay and disunity, King Stanislaus II of Poland was unable to resist annexation by his neighbors. The Polish uprising in 1794 in response to the French Revolution, and the reactionary response of the conservative crown, led to the third and final division of the country that eliminated Poland altogether from the map.

In the War of Bavarian Succession (1778-1779), Friedrich again defeated Austria to prevent its annexation of Bavaria. In 1778, he created the "League of Princes" (*Fürstenbund*) to replace the Austrian Hapsburgs as the primary dynasty in the Holy Roman Empire. The League represented the first organization of German states under the leadership of Prussia, which in 1871 unified Germany under the Hohenzollern monarchy.

The Tragedy of Empire

The "tragedy of empire" unfolding in Germany over the next century and a half after the death of Friedrich the Great, and ending with the collapse of the Hohenzollern monarchy after WWI, and of the Third German Empire (*Dritte Reich*) after WWII has two probable roots. One is the diminishing ability of the Prussian rulers after Friedrich the Great. The other root is the systemic violence inherent in empire built not only on suppression of the monarch's own people, but the expansion of state power and territory at the expense of foreign populations.

Since Friedrich II had no children of his own, the throne fell to his brother's son, for whom the King did not have much respect. Friedrich-Wilhelm II (ruled 1786-1797) was a libertine, whose lavish and expensive lifestyle emptied the state treasury. His first marriage, to a cousin, ended in divorce because of adultery. A second wife bore him eight children, but she was forced to accept two bigamist families which produced additional children.

With the outbreak of the French Revolution (1789-1794), King Friedrich-Wilhelm II joined the Coalition of European Powers to restore the Bourbon dynasty, but in 1795 his financial difficulties forced him to make a separate, humiliating, peace with France.

His son, King Friedrich-Wilhelm III (1794-1840) did not fare much better. Hoping to avoid the Napoleonic juggernaut, the morally earnest and religious, but irresolute, King assumed a stance of neutrality. Urgent calls for military reform from Barons von Stein, Hardenberg, Gneisenau and Scharnhorst, fell on deaf ears. Once Napoleon overran Germany, however, the King had no choice but to declare war. By that time, Prussia had not fought a battle in over a decade, and the army was ill prepared.

The twin battles at Jena and Auerstedt on October 14, 1806 proved disastrous for the Prussians. They fielded twice as many soldiers as did the French, but suffered four times the losses. The King and Queen fled to the easternmost part of the kingdom. At the Peace of Tilsit (1807) Napoleon imposed harsh terms, took control of the western half of Prussia and imposed annual reparations equal to the entire Prussian budget, essentially reducing the kingdom to a vassal state. The King sent his wife to Tilsit to beg for a better settlement, but Napoleon refused, mocking the Queen, saying that she was "the last man left standing in Prussia" (Herold, 2002, 177). The shame of Jena-Auerstedt became the foundation of nineteenth-century German nationalism. After the Prussian defeat, Napoleon forced more than three hundred principalities into the Confederation of the Rhine, which eventually included thirty six states, to form a buffer between France and Austria and Bavaria.

Culturally, the Confederation made a huge impact. The idea of Germany as a nation of people sharing the same language and traditions came to be articulated in socio-political movements, philosophy, poetry and fiction, in linguistic, ethnographic and folklore

studies and collections, intended to save the traditions of the German "folk" from being lost to rapid industrialization and urbanization.

Politically, however, could things get any worse? The Prussian heir, Friedrich-Wilhelm IV (1844-57), was a mentally unstable mystic who yearned to return to a paternalistic monarchy of medieval structure. When social revolts broke out in Prussia in March, 1848, he dissolved the Constituent Assembly and promulgated a reactionary constitution to safeguard the primacy of absolute monarchy.

By May of the same year, a National Assembly in Frankfurt was called by German liberals elected by direct vote from the entire political spectrum. By March 1849 the Assembly adopted a federal constitution of all the German states, and offered the office of hereditary German Emperor to Friedrich-Wilhelm. However, he refused to accept the crown from the hands of a popularly elected body, thereby ending the first effort to unify Germany democratically. The King's own plan to unify Germany under Prussian leadership foundered on Austrian opposition.

By 1857, the King's mental condition had deteriorated to the point that he was replaced by his brother who ruled as regent until crowned King as Wilhelm I (1861-1888) upon his predecessor's death.

Wilhelm, who had fled to England during the revolutionary uprisings of 1848, upon his return crushed the republican insurrection in Baden and set out to reform the army. More importantly, he appointed Otto von Bismarck prime minister, who in effect became the political leader of Prussia and eventually of imperial Germany as chancellor. In the Austro-Prussian War (1866), Bismarck defeated Denmark to annex Schleswig-Holstein; in the Franco-Prussia War (1870-1871), he defeated Napoleon III and declared the Second German Empire under the Hohenzollern crown, firmly committed to the idea of divine right rule. He passed legislation to suppress socialist impulses toward constitutional monarchy.

Dropping the Pilot, cartoon by John Tenniell (*Punch*), 1890

Wilhelm I's son, Friedrich III, ruled for only ninety nine days before he died from throat cancer. As crown prince he had married the daughter of British Queen Victoria with whom he shared a liberal ideology, hoping to unify Germany by peaceful means, but it was Bismarck's policy of "Iron and Blood" (*Eisen und Blut*) expressed in his speech in 1862 to the **Prussian House of Representatives** that prevailed: "The position of Prussia in Germany will not be determined by its liberalism but by its power … Not through speeches and majority decisions will the great questions of the day be decided—but by "iron and blood" (Hollyday, 1970, 16-18).

Friedrich III's hope to make the Empire more liberal was not shared by his son, Wilhelm II, the last German emperor. Wilhelm, who suffered from a withered arm perhaps due to **cerebral palsy**, held none of his parents' liberal ideas and as crown prince was set by Bismarck on a collision course with his parents. Once Emperor, his impulsive love of military display probably rooted in a sense of inferiority from his physical impairment, soon created conflicts with his pragmatic chancellor. Bismarck, who had effectively ruled Prussia and Germany for over thirty years, was forced to resign in 1890.

Without the chancellor's steady hand to guide his vague aspirations to build Germany's naval power and colonial possessions, the Emperor neglected the alliance with Russia that Bismarck had forged, and blundered into WWI in alliance with Austria, Italy and Turkey. With the Alliance's defeat, the Hohenzollern dynasty collapsed, followed by naval mutiny, civilian revolt and republican proclamations in major German cities.

Friedrich the Great?

The majority of nineteenth century historians glorified Friedrich II as the romantic model of the great warrior and capable monarch. He built Prussia into a dominant European power and laid the foundations of the German Empire. During the twelve years of Nazi rule (1933-45), Hitler idolized the King as the greatest German leader ever. Most Prussians (and Germans) today hold a more critical view of the "Great Warrior" (Abott, 2017).

From the start, the expansion of Prussia's might involved violent suppression of non-German indigenous populations: Celts, Wends, Slavs, Sorbs, Old Prussians, Kashubians, Lithuanians, Baltics, Bohemians, Russians, and many other minorities. Of course, the suppression of native populations was not unique to Prussia and can be found anywhere in the world wherever empires are built, from ancient Rome and the empire of Alexander the Great, to the colonization of North and South America, Africa and Asia by Portugal, Belgium, Spain, the Netherlands, and England, or most recently in the world-wide capitalist hegemony of the U.S., or the Marxist dictatorships of the Soviet Union and Communist China.

However, the violence of empire building becomes all the more egregious when carried out in the name of religion. What some modern Catholic theologians today call the "Universal Christ," C. G. Jung referred to as the archetype of "Universal Love" breaking into European consciousness during the early Middle Ages (Wright, 2001, 6-8). But the story of Europe's conversion to the Christian deity is mostly one of violent empire building. The Ostrogoths were probably the only Germanic tribe to be converted peacefully, by one of their own, the Arian priest Wulfilas (Sehmsdorf, 2020, 45f). By 325 AD, Emperor Constantine, in accepting Christianity as the state religion of Rome, irreversibly fused the interests of the Empire with state-authorized faith. In the

Allegory of the first partition of Poland, showing Catherine the Great of Russia, Joseph II of Austria and Friedrich the Great of Prussia quarreling with the king of Poland over their territorial seizures.

German North, Charlemagne in 742 AD cemented the expansion of the Frankish Empire by decapitating some four thousand Saxon chieftains who refused baptism, thereby ending Saxon resistance to his authority. Likewise half a millennium later, the Teutonic Knights, sworn to Christ by their monastic vows, exterminated the Old Prussians who stubbornly resisted giving up their native deities. The Brandenburg rulers from the Great Elector to the Great Friedrich practiced religious tolerance as long as it didn't interfere with their expansionist policies, but as late as during the nineteenth century, Bismarck waged "culture war" (*Kulturkampf*) against the Catholic Church which represented 36.5% of the population, including millions of Poles, for the sake of strengthening the political power of the state. Half of the Catholic bishops in Prussia

were imprisoned or exiled, many monasteries and convents closed, parishes left without priests and lay people put into jail.

In absolute monarchies, the religious and civic rights of subjects were specifically limited by the divine rights of the King in law or in political practice. The American Constitution of 1779 guarantees the life, liberty and property rights of every citizen, an ideal of personal freedom that was not fully realized in Prussia for another century. In 1807 Prussia abolished serfdom on crown lands and noble estates, giving freedom to peasants and ownership of half or two-thirds of the lands they were working. Expanded civil and human rights were introduced in Prussia during the revolution of 1848-1849, but reactionary monarchs struck some of these rights from the constitutional text or neutralized them administratively. The Northern German Confederation restored many of the individual rights secured by the Prussian constitution, and in 1869 Jews were formally enfranchised as citizens.

The progressive dismemberment of the dual monarchy of the Kingdom of Poland and the Grand Duchy of Lithuania provides the most violent example of suppression of ethnicities, and of their cultures and languages, in the tragic arc of expansionist empire building and its aftermath.

The partitions were conducted between 1772 and 1795 by the Habsburg Monarchy, the Kingdom of Prussia, and the Russian Empire, who progressively divided up the Polish-Lithuanian Commonwealth by territorial seizures and annexations, eventually resulting in the elimination of sovereign Poland and Lithuania for more than a century. During the Napoleonic Wars the borders between partitioning powers shifted several times, but by the time the Congress of Vienna (1815) restored the European monarchies, Russia controlled 82% of the former Commonwealth's territory, Austria 11%, and Prussia 7%.

King Stanisław II August (1764-95) was the last monarch of the Polish–Lithuanian Commonwealth. His attempts to liberalize the monarchy and mitigate the worst abuses of serfdom, were met with intervention by his absolutist neighbors, resulting in the first partition in 1772. The Commonwealth lost about 30% of its territory and half of its population, including Ukrainians, Bello-Russians, Ruthenian Slavs, and other minorities. Prussia gained control over 80% of the Commonwealth's foreign trade, and the enormous custom duties levied by Prussia accelerated the Commonwealth's economic collapse.

Already in 1791, the Polish King had pushed through parliamentary adoption of a constitution to establish a monarchic republic with divided executive, legislative, and judiciary powers. This was in effect Europe's first modern constitution modeled on the American Constitution (1789). But the reforms were opposed by territorial landlords and barons, and again neighboring monarchs intervened, leading to the second partition of Poland (1793), which left only one-third of the population in Poland. Prussia named its newly gained province South Prussia, with Posen (today Poznán) as its capital.

In 1794, a Polish veteran of the American Revolutionary War spearheaded a general uprising to "regain the independence of the nation, and to strengthen universal liberties" (Storozynsky 2009, 180-181). Again the three neighboring monarchies intervened, leading to the third partition (1795) of the Commonwealth. Prussia ended up with 20% of the Commonwealth's population, Austria with 18%, and Russia with 62%.

Prussia Germanized the entire school system, showing little regard for Polish language, culture and institutions. Countless Polish noblemen, politicians, writers, and artists fled to become revolutionaries in 19th-century Europe, and four million Poles emigrated to the U.S. A hundred and twenty-three years later, after WWI, the Treaty of Versailles finally restored Poland's full independence in the German territories of West Prussia, Posen and Upper Silesia.

However, yet another partition of Poland occurred during WWII by the German–Soviet Pact (1939–1941). The pact was rescinded when Germany declared war on the Soviet Union, ultimately leading to its own defeat in 1945. After the war, the victorious Allies parceled out all German provinces east of the Oder River, about a quarter of all territory Germany had held by 1937. The Soviets took East Prussia (where both my father and I were born), Poland took the City of Danzig (where my mother was born), Pomerania, and Western Silesia, and Czechoslovakia got a sliver of Upper Silesia, pending a final settlement under a future peace treaty that would formally end the war.

It was also decided to expel all ethnic Germans from central and Eastern Europe, and resettle them west of the Oder "in an orderly and humane manner" (*Potsdam Agreement: Protocol*, 1945). It is estimated that the expulsions uprooted 12-14 million persons, and that about 2.6 million died during the forced marches to the West. About 20% of the citizens of Germany today are descendants of the millions forced to leave their homes and properties in Eastern Europe after 1945. While the signatories of the Potsdam Agreement considered the expulsions legal under international law, intended to prevent future conflicts if sizable German minorities remained within the boundaries of East European nations, today they are mostly thought of as acts of ethnic cleansing that violated the human rights of the affected populations. As recently as in 2018, German Chancellor Angela Merkel, speaking at the U.N. World Refuge Day, questioned the "moral or political justification" for the post-war expulsions. Three years later, at the opening of the Documentation Center for Displacement,

Expulsion, and Reconciliation in Berlin, Merkel called the German expulsions in the aftermath of WWII "an injustice" (Merkel, 2021).

In 1947, the Allies also abolished Prussia as a state because they saw it as the leading German aggressor inflaming Nazism. After the fall of the Berlin Wall in 1989, the German–Polish Border Treaty acknowledged the post-war boundary along the Oder-Neisse line as permanent, thus renouncing any German claims to the former Prussian territories in Silesia, East Brandenburg, Farther Pomerania, and East Prussia. The subsequent German–Polish Treaty of Good Neigborship supplemented the Border Treaty to ensure certain rights for political minorities on either side of the border. Today census figures place the total number of ethnic Germans still living in Eastern Europe at approximately 2.6 million, about 12% of the pre-war total. While so-called "Imperial Burghers" (*Reichsbürger*) in Germany still cling to the idea of recovering the lost territories, by legal or by violent means, the policy of the German Federal Republic enshrined in its constitution is to live in peace and harmony with its neighbors: "Activities tending and undertaken with the intent to disturb peaceful relations between nations, especially to prepare for aggressive war, are unconstitutional" (Article 26). The high-arching trajectory of empire embodied in the tragic history of Prussia and imperial Germany has finally fallen back to earth.

The Idea of Prussia

What does the idea of "homeland" (*Heimatland*) mean to a Prussian today? Who would call himself Prussian, given that no territory or state by that name exists any more? I was born in Königsberg, founded in 1255 by the Teutonic Knights, the capital of their monastic state, which became the Duchy of Prussia, and the province of East Prussia until 1701, when the Prussian capital was moved to Berlin. Königsberg was the easternmost large city in Germany until WWII. Heavily damaged by Allied bombing in 1944, it was annexed by the Soviet Union in 1945, its German population expelled and replaced by Russians. Renamed Kaliningrad, the city became the capital of the Kaliningrad Oblast, a Baltic exclave of what is now Russia.

Königsberg. Engraving by Friedrich Bernhard Werner, ca. 1750

However, over the course of its 700-year existence, Königsberg had developed into a multicultural city. While predominantly German-speaking, the city also profoundly influenced Lithuanian and Polish culture. Some of the first books in those languages were published. in Königsberg. Its university, founded in 1544 as the second oldest Protestant academy, made Königsberg into an intellectual and cultural center, where thinkers, writers, and artists flourished. Major names on a short list include: Simon Dach (1605-59), poet and Lutheran hymn writer; E.T.A. Hoffman (1776-1822), Romantic author and composer, whose stories were set to music by Tchaikovsky, Offenbach, and Schumann; Immanuel Kant (1724-1804), whose ground-breaking works in epistemology, metaphysics, ethics, and

Alexander and Wilhelm von Humboldt in conversation with Goethe and Schiller, 1797

aesthetics made him one of the most significant Western thinkers; David Hilbert (1862-1943), mathematician and physicist who laid the foundations of quantum mechanics; Käthe Kollwitz (1867-1945), Expressionist painter, lithographer and sculptor who castigated the effects of war, poverty, and hunger especially on the working class; Agnes Migel (1879-1964), poet and short story writer, a supporter of the Nazi regime, who after the war mostly wrote about East Prussia, the lost land of her youth; Hannah Arendt (1906-1975), Jewish-American philosopher best known for her writings about totalitarian power and evil; and part-Jewish violinist and author Michael Wieck (1928-2021), best remembered for his memoir *Witness to the Fall of Königsberg* (Wieck, 1989), which describes his family's suffering, first under the Nazis, and then the Soviets.

If we look beyond Königsberg to Prussia as a whole, a nearly endless list of luminaries crowd the pages of the cultural history, from Alexander Humboldt (1769-1859), polymath, geographer, explorer and Romantic philosopher and scientist, to his brother Wilhelm (1767-1835), linguist, philosopher, Prussian diplomat and founder of the

Humboldt University of Berlin; Günther Grass (1927-2015) German novelist, poet, playwright, illustrator, graphic artist, sculptor, recipient of the 1999 Nobel Prize in Literature, and author of the unforgettable *Tin Drum* (Blechtrommel), a persiflage of the Nazi experience seen through the eyes of a little boy confined to an insane asylum; and Paul Tillich (1886-1965), existentialist philosopher widely regarded as one of the most influential theologians of the twentieth century. Tillich, with whom I studied at the University of Chicago, had profound influence on my own spiritual development, as did all the other Prussian thinkers and artists listed. Would not any Prussian take pride in that creative ancestry?

The culture of German Prussia started with the Teutonic Knights who drained swamps and wetlands and cleared forest to create fertile fields and established monasteries as centers of learning, and towns that became thriving commercial centers. My oldest known ancestor lived in Old Prussia twenty-one generations ago. Gerhard von Wickbold was a city councillor in Kolberg (today Kołobrzeg, Poland) from 1282 to 1290, about the time when the Teutonic Knights took control of the Baltic shore previously settled by a mix of Slavic tribes. During the fifth-sixth centuries, Pomeranians had settled by the shore of the Baltic Sea between the mouths of the Oder and the Weichsel rivers, replacing indigenous Celtic peoples, and after them Gothic tribes. By the time the Teutonic Knights arrived in 1309, the people of Kolberg had already been Christianized for nearly a century.

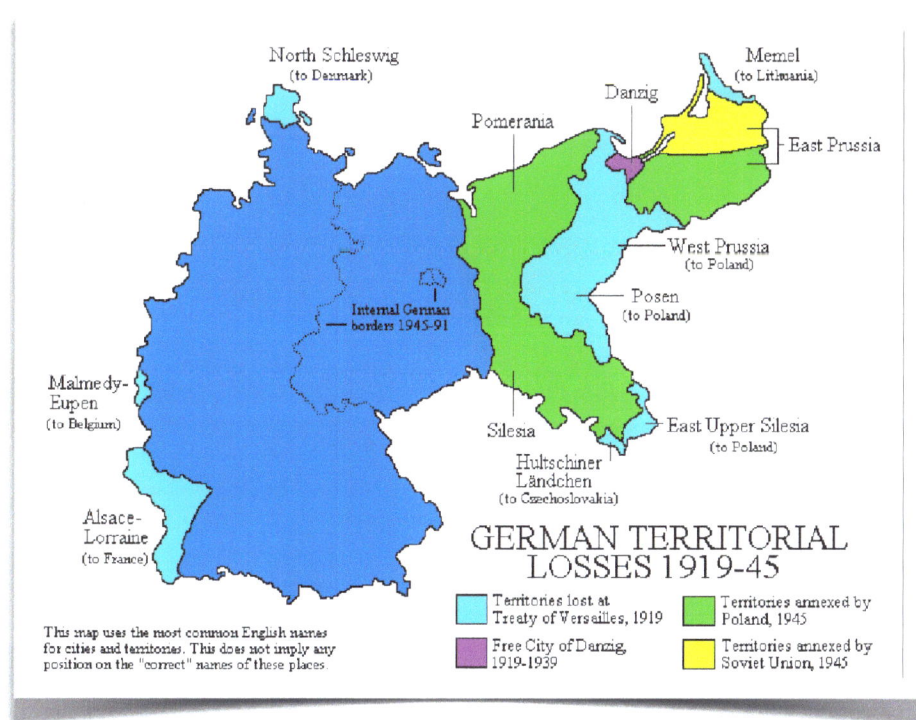

GERMAN TERRITORIAL LOSSES 1919-45

This map uses the most common English names for cities and territories. This does not imply any position on the "correct" names of these places.

- Territories lost at Treaty of Versailles, 1919
- Free City of Danzig, 1919-1939
- Territories annexed by Poland, 1945
- Territories annexed by Soviet Union, 1945

The cultural codes later termed Prussian virtues (*preußische Tugenden*), had their source in the religious vows of the Teutonic Order. Originally the monastic vows focused on obedience to God under the authority of Rome. After the secularization of the Teutonic states, these values were reshaped by the Calvinism of the absolutist Prussian rulers, and came to be associated both with the cultural standards of the Prussian nobility and of the middle classes. The frugal "Soldier King" saw himself as a moral role model for his administrators and subjects, and his Enlightenment-era son, Friedrich the Great, aspired to ethnic, linguistic and religious tolerance in governing a diverse state that was home to Germans, Poles, Lithuanians, and Sorbs, Protestants, Catholics and Jews. Especially after the Prussian defeat at the hand of Napoleon, the Hohenzollern dynasty sought to strengthen a common sense of patriotism in support of the King ruling by divine right. As Prussia grew in power within Germany, its behavioral codes significantly expanded to shape the wider German culture, all the way to the contemporary German standards of efficiency, austerity and discipline.

Prussian virtues were decidedly paternalistic. From the King styled as *pater patriae* (*Landesvater*), to the *pater familias* (*Familienvater)*, the male head of the household exercised legal authority over his wife and children. On both levels of society, paternal authority was linked to the will of God, as expressed in the much quoted poem by Ludwig Hölty (1748–1776), in which filial loyalty and honesty are equated with "the way of God" (Hölty, 1776). Set to music by Mozart from a theme adapted from his *Magic Flute*, the melody was played every day on the bells over the grave of Friedrich the Great at the garrison church in Potsdam.

The exercise of authority in the name of the divine order, however, becomes problematic when not balanced by human sympathy, kindness, patience, and understanding. The Teutonic Knights suppressed recalcitrant pagans in Old Prussia refusing baptism, by dispossessing them of their land, even killing them, thus failing to heed the fundamental command of Christian faith to "love your neighbor as yourself." Centuries later, the Soldier King cruelly abused his recalcitrant son when the crown prince tried to run away from his duties as future ruler. A strict and austere Calvinist, Friedrich Wilhelm II acted from conviction that not to hold the prince responsible for desertion would undo the principle of justice in his realm. However, in his towering rage he failed to show any measure of sympathetic understanding for the suffering of the teenage prince. Many a Prussian father beat his disobedient children to bend them to a behavioral code authorized by the example of the divine right ruler. Thus every Prussian virtue potentially shaded into its opposite, and turned into vice.

The Prussian virtues (as I experienced them in my own family) could be grouped into several overlapping categories: justice, obedience, loyalty, fortitude, discipline, and work ethic. Neither my parents nor grandparents on either side of the family were devout Christians, although they insisted on being baptized as Lutherans, as befitted loyal Prussians. Their sense of justice, however, was religious in the sense that being "just" meant conforming to established spiritual law. In contrast to the Anglo-American understanding of justice based on legal precedent — past decisions or cases acting as standards for future decisions — the Prussian concept of justice was based on absolute legal standards encoded in The General Laws for the Prussian States (*Allgemeines Landrecht für die Preußischen Staaten*, 1794), under the orders of Friedrich II (Hattenau, 1970). The code had over 17,000 articles covering civil, penal, family, public, and administrative law. As part of family law, the code gave men absolute authority over wives and children, and thus fathers became arbiters of justice in the family. In 1900, Prussian *Landrecht* was replaced by a common civil code (*Bürgerliches Gesetzbuch*, abbreviated *BGB*) for the whole of the German Empire. As a lawyer, my father often referenced the *BGB* — a huge gold-leaf leather volume residing on a bookshelf in his study — when couching his expectations of proper behavior on the part of his family in terms of law.

Justice (*Gerechtigkeitssinn*), incorruptibility (*Unbestechlichkeit*), reliability (*Zuverlässigkeit*), restraint (*Zurückhaltung*), self-denial (*Selbstverleugnung*), conscientiousness (*Pflichtbewußtsein*), or sense of order (*Ordnungssinn*), didn't just mean right behavior, but a sense of knowing one's place in the social order.

The virtue of obedience (*Gehorsam*) was tied to loyalty (*Treue*), subordination (*Unterordnung*), and discipline (*Disziplin*). These virtues are the most ambiguous in Prussian mentality, fraught with potential abuse in public and in private life.

As a schoolboy, I loved to sing "I had a Comrade"(*Ich hatt' einen Kameraden*), a text written by Ludwig Uhland in 1809 and set to music in 1825 based on a Swiss folk song (Oesterle, 1958). Later I learned that the song had become a traditional funeral lament of the German armed forces and been adopted by the militaries of Austria, France, Spain, the Netherlands, South America, Japan, and elsewhere for its timeless and apolitical expression of a soldier's losing a loyal comrade,

The Good Comrade. War Memorial, Speyer, Rhineland-Palatinate

"as if he were a part of me." Whenever the song is played, attending soldiers are expected to salute, an honor normally reserved for the national anthem. In Germany, the song is played at Remembrance Day (*Volkstrauertag*) at memorials for the war dead. Anti-war playwright Carl Zuckmayer used the same line as the title of his autobiography (Zuckmayer, 1966).

In Prussian tradition, loyalty and obedience were tied to "blood" in reference to family and ethnic identity, a use of the term that has roots dating back to Greek and Roman traditions. The term is reflected in the German proverb that "blood is thicker than water," a proverb first stated in the Medieval trickster tales of Reynard the Fox (*Reinhard der Fuchs*, 1180, by Heinrich der Gleißner. Kürschner, 2009). A derivation is the popular custom of "blood brothers" pledging mutual loyalty in a ceremony of exchanging blood. As an adolescent I entered a friendship with a fellow student who, I felt, would be my brother for life, "as if he were part of me." I harbor similar to feelings toward my spouse and my children even today.

However, the connection of "blood" to loyalty and obedience also had its shadow side. My father shocked me later in life when we found ourselves in moral conflict, and he accused me of "blood treason." Analogously, during the fateful twelve years of National Socialist rule (1933-1945), German people in all walks of life were required to swear a blood oath of loyalty and obedience (*Treue und Gehorsam*) to Adolf Hitler. Anyone refusing to swear the loyalty oath was fired from his job and lost their social position, or worse. For example, Dietrich Bonhoeffer, Prussian aristocrat and Lutheran pastor, and founder of the Confessing Church (*Bekennende Kirche*) in opposition to the Nazis, was tortured to death by hanging with barbed wire for refusing to swear loyalty to Hitler.

In 1767, Friedrich II had published *Memoirs of the House of Brandenburg* (Memoires pour Servir a l'Histoire de la Maison de Brandebourg), in which he told how the Prince of Homburg in an unauthorized attack on the Swedish enemy won the battle at Fehrbellin (1675), but was judged insubordinate to the will of the Great Elector. Friedrich identified Homburg's refusal to defer to his royal superior with his own conflict in defying his own father's trying to force him to succeed to the Prussian crown as ordained by "blood."

Heinrich von Kleist (1777-1801) dramatized the clash of obedience and self-willed passion in the psychological play *The Prince of Homburg* (Prinz Friedrich von Homburg, 1809-1810). Because of the controversial battle between reason and insubordination in the lead character, the play could not be published during the dramatist's lifetime, and its performance subsequently was repeatedly forbidden by the royal house (Tieck, 1821).

Closely related to obedience, discipline and subordination are the virtues of courage (*Mut)*, fortitude (*Tapferkeit)*, toughness (*Härte)*, and attitude (*Haltung)*. The ideal virtues my family held up before the children, especially the boys, was that we become "Fast as whippets, tough as leather, and hard as Krupp steel" (*Schnell wie Windhunde, zäh wie Leder und hart wie Kruppstahl)*. Courage was seen as cheerful acceptance of difficulties, and fortitude meant to "learn to suffer without complaining" (*Lerne leiden ohne zu klagen)*, for example, when our rough and tumble play resulted in injuries, or when we thought we had been treated unfairly. Proper attitude was seen not only as positive feeling or mood, but also as physical posture manifesting inner strength and respect. Communication between the generations was respectful and formal, rather than playful, intimate or confiding, and slouching around was frowned upon. A bored child was thought to have the wrong attitude and was given a corrective task.

In the context of these ideal behaviors, it often became difficult for a child like myself to practice another set of often stated virtues, namely frankness (*Redlichkeit)*, humility (*Bescheidenheit)*, sincerity (*Aufrichtigkeit)*, or straightforwardness (*Geradlinigkeit)*. My extraverted siblings had an easier time with these behavioral codes because their actions and what came out of their mouths was usually in line with how they felt about themselves and the world. By contrast, an inward-turned child like myself found it difficult to be open and straightforward, to act on or speak about feelings not condoned by the adults.

The Prussian virtues that have survived into contemporary Germany are austerity or thrift (*Sparsamkeit)*, determination (*Zielstrebigkeit)*, industriousness (*Fleiß)*, and punctuality (*Pünktlichkeit)*. The German economist Max Weber in his epochal **The Protestant Ethic and the Spirit of Capitalism** (*Die Protestantische Ethik und der Geist des Kapitalismus*, 1904-1905; Weber, 2002) argued that the work ethic espoused by the Prussian kings' emphasizing frugality, discipline and diligence are the secular result of the Protestant faith. Specifically, the Calvinist doctrine of asceticism and predestination enabled the rise of capitalism. Martin Luther had cast work as duty to benefit society as a whole, but Calvinists taught that only the predestined would be saved; therefore diligent work, frugality, and determination came to be regarded as signs of being among the elect. This idea came to define not only European, but to a degree also American society.

During WWII, traditional Prussian virtues were turned on their heads and their shadow sides emerged into full view. "Cadaverous" military obedience and subordination (*Kadavergehorsam)* became the expected norm for society. Obedience was enforced from the political center by a dictatorial regime, replacing the *pater patriae* serving the welfare of his people. Efficiency, discipline and the work ethic became tools of subjugation and eventually of the Holocaust. Ironically, after the end of the war, the very same qualities made rebuilding the devastated country possible.

Culturally, however, after the War, Germans were increasingly consumed with seeking atonement for their collective responsibility for the destructive horrors of the war. By the time of the German student protests in 1968, a new generation was ready to reject all traditional values thought to have enabled the rise of militarism in any form. Not just in Germany, but in Western philosophy, the arts, literature and culture in general, post-modernist thought radically questioned the certainties generally accepted before the two world wars. Statements pretending to universal truth were systematically deconstructed as ideologies intended to assert and maintain political and economic power (H. Sehmsdorf, 2023).

And yet, the virtues associated with the idea of Prussia continue to remain effective in the world. The other day my wife read to me a passage from a book about a group of men exploring the length of the Amazon. The leader of the group was a Pole, born and raised in the same area that once was Prussia, and had passed repeatedly back and forth between German and Polish control, an area which for a long time shared a common cultural heritage in spite of ethnic and linguistic differences and mutual hostilities. In listening to the story of this man, who came from a large and poor family, I was struck by how closely the values he modeled for his teammates on this dangerous adventure reflected the best of the Prussian virtues. It was these values that made him the natural leader of the expedition. He was tough and austere but forbearing, suffered hardship without complaint, was disciplined but patient, frank and sincere without harshness, and he loyally subordinated his own needs to those of the group. He explained these values as deeply imbedded in the culture from which he came:

"Everyone had a specific role, a place, well-defined duties within the structure of the family and community. In that poor and troubled country one's dignity was found in the performance of those duties… [This is] easy to do when everyone feels good. When feeling bad, rules tell you what to do. When it is my turn to perform a task, it does not matter how I feel. I do not have my own life."

The author of the book, a member of the expedition, admitted frankly that at first the Pole's attitude was not something he appreciated:

"From my corner of the New World, from my culture of abused abundance, I regarded the preoccupation with duty and manners and prescribed social roles as a weapon of the powerful few, the invoking of arcane forms for the purpose of intimidation" (Kane, 1990).

But as the six-month voyage of death-defying travel over four thousand miles down the river unfolded, it became abundantly clear that without the selflessness and courage of their leader putting the needs of the group before his own comfort, this polyglot assembly of urbanized travelers would have failed to overcome their fear and egotism, and perhaps would not have survived the journey.

Hearing this, I thought to myself: Now here is a virtuous Prussian — and he is a Pole!

Mother's Family :
Rathenow, Braunsberg, Danzig, Thorn, and Wehlau

Rathenow

The patrilineal side of my mother's family is closely tied to the ancient town of Rathenow, today a thriving city and administrative center of the Haveland district in western Brandenburg, with a population of twenty-six thousand. Archeologists documented settlements of fishermen, hunters and gatherers of unknown origin in the Havel River watershed as early as 10,000 BC. By 3500 BC, permanent agriculturalists were raising plants and animals in the area, and making ceramics. During the Bronze Age after 1700 BC, copper came into use for weapons, jewelry and tools, and by 500 BC, the use of iron became common.

As reported by Graeco-Roman authors, by 12 BC the Semnones, a Germanic tribe, settled the Havel watershed, but were driven south during the Germanic migrations (400-600 AD) by Slavic Wends arriving from the east. Between 800-950 AD, the Wends established large-scale fortifications that became the foundation of Old Rathenow, first mentioned as a town in 1216 in a document by Siegfried II, Bishop of Brandenburg. The area was eventually reached by Saxons coming from the west, who in 782 AD had been forcibly Christianized by Charlemagne at the battle of Verden (today Verdun, France). In 785 Charlemagne captured Widukind, the last Saxon leader to rival his power, thereby ending resistance to Christianity among the Saxons. The new Saxon arrivals at the Havel intermarried with the indigenous Slavs, though ethnic distinctions remained, notably in regard to religion, with the Slavs continuing to worship their native deities.

In 1220, a Romanesque cruciform basilica was built in Rathenow. In 1288 the settlement was given jurisdiction by the Margrave, i.e., it received authority to hear court cases and determine local law. In 1295, a formal town charter was granted and Margrave Otto IV deeded the village Jederitz and its surrounding fields to the town.

From the thirteenth century on, the administration of Rathenow lay in the hands of a town council headed by a mayor, originally subordinate to a bailiff (*Vogt* or *Schultheiß*) appointed by the Margrave. The mayors were originally chosen by the bailiff from among the leading burghers of the town, but eventually they came to be elected directly by the town council. By the seventeenth-eighteenth centuries, the office of mayor routinely became a civil service appointment.

A burgher (*Bürger* from Old High German *burgari*, originally a dweller of a fortified place or castle, a *burg*), was any legally recognized male inhabitant of the town. In contrast to the feudal serfs working the fields of the landowning nobility, a burgher was a free man making his living within the town limits, richer and more influential than a peasant or unskilled worker. Thus the growth of towns like Rathenow represented a profound shift in collective mentality, founded on the transition to an economy based on money, in contrast to an economy based on land ownership. Mostly, burghers were merchants or craftsmen allowed to trade in town free of charge. They could obtain these rights by inheritance, marriage, purchase, or gift. In the civic hierarchy of Rathenow, the leading citizens were well-to-do house owners and members of the craft guilds: master bakers, butchers, brewers, cloth makers, tailors and glove makers. All of this is duly noted in my Mother's family's genealogical records (Müller, n.d.).

By 1539, the House of Brandenburg accepted the Protestant Reformation. In 1555 at the Peace of Augusburg, the Protestant princes of the North and the Catholic of the South agreed on the principle of *cuius regio eius religio* ("whose territory, his religion"), meaning that a population was obliged to accept the faith of its ruler. Religious freedom as personal choice as promised in Luther's reading of the New Testament was not an option in the political context of the widening rivalry between the Catholic Empire and Protestant rulers. By 1540 Rathenow was home to 2,500 residents, but during the Thirty Years' War (1618-1648), the town was repeatedly ransacked by Swedish, Brandenburg and Imperial troops, and by the end of the war its population had shrunk to no more than 40 survivors.

The Great Elector, Friedrich-Wilhelm (1620-1688), systematically rebuilt the population of Brandenburg by promoting immigration from France, the Netherlands, other regions of Germany, Switzerland, and Austria. By 1662, many of the scattered inhabitants of Rathenow had returned, and the town council rebuilt the Brickworks destroyed during the war, a public enterprise of central importance to the economy of the town, where most of the buildings were constructed of brick. The leaseholder (*Pächter*) who ran the Brickworks thus occupied an elevated social position in the town.

Between 1720-1740, Rathenow erected toll gates in the ancient fortifications surrounding the town to establish a tariff wall controlling the flow of goods in and out of the town. Among the products exported from Rathenow were woven cloth and leather goods, shoes, gloves and clothing. The local food supply was provided by bakers, butchers, carp seiners, brewers and ploughmen (*Ackermann*) employed by the town to work the fields outside the fortification walls. By 1744, the town was home to a population of 3,820 and boasted twenty-two breweries. In the 1780s, the largest food depot for the Prussian military was

established on an island on the Havel River adjacent to Rathenow, which became a major garrison town.

The craft guilds, which had emerged in the Middle Ages as a counterweight to the power of the feudal nobility, were associations of tradesmen, formed to protect mutual interests and maintain product quality standards. Members were ranked as masters, journeymen, and apprentices. Only masters were allowed to sell product, train apprentices, or have employees. To become a master one would have to complete an apprenticeship, then serve several years as a journeyman working for another master at home or abroad, and produce an acceptable master work. One would also have to be a burgher of the community, requiring an entry fee to the guild. The status of burghers was thus distinct from that of other residents of a community. A burgher was entitled to full municipal rights entailing participation in the government, certain judicial rights, and the freedom to trade. A burgher also had social standing above the rest of the community. The children of masters enjoyed reduced guild fees, which led to the continuity of particular trades in families. Clergy and employees of the feudal ruler were exempted from these regulations.

Among my mother's twenty male ancestors hailing from Rathenow over six generations (1663-1837), there were seven master cloth makers, four master tailors, two master glove makers and one master button maker, eight master brewers, two master innkeepers, two master bakers and one master ploughman. There were also three leaseholders of the Town Brickworks. Most of these men practiced multiple trades: baker and brewer, brewer and innkeeper, cloth maker and tailor, glove and button maker, and in most instances the trades were passed from father to son. Twelve out of the twenty were home owners, and seven were city councillors. Their wives, although they most certainly participated in the men's trades in important ways, are listed only as spouses.

The first direct ancestor of my mother's documented among notables of Rathenow was Brickworks leaseholder Johann Christian Seiffarth (born in 1754). He was known by the sobriquet "very noble" (*hochedler*), which title, however, did not mean that he was a nobleman, but that as the person who had

Rathenow City Hall and houses of burghers, 1887

administrative and managerial authority over the Town Brickworks, he held an important position in the civic life of Rathenow.

In the early 1840s, another upward social shift occurred in my mother's family. Master baker Carl Ferdinand Seyffarth (1808-1883), decided to send his son Carl Wilhelm Ferdinand Seyffarth (1839-1904) — my great-grandfather — to the Upper Burgher School (*Gehobene Bürgerschule*) in Rathenow. Such schools were established at the initiative of the Margrave to educate state administrators. Upon graduation from that school, the boy qualified to attend the Latin School (*Gymnasium*) in the capital of Brandenburg, and then to study law at the university in Berlin. The momentous

Danzig at the end of the 19th century

decision to provide the boy with an education beyond what was needed to continue in the family trades, fundamentally changed his relationship to his native town and to the historical position of the family in Rathenow's economic and social hierarchy. It meant that

the young man spent much of his adolescence away from the family. Nor did he return home to Rathenow after becoming a lawyer. Instead he took public service in the judicial system of the state of Brandenburg, eventually rising to the office of regional court judge in the medieval town of Braunsberg (town charter, 1284), in Eastern Prussia (Polish Braniewo). In 1871, at age thirty-two, he married my great-grandmother, Martha Katharina Therese Starkowski (born 1844). She descended from five generations of master shoemakers, brewers, city councillors and mayor of Rosenberg (Polish Susz), and as many generations of fishermen, carp pond owners (*Karpfenseigner*), marine navigator, innkeepers, and burghers in the city of Danzig (Polish Gdansk).

By choosing higher education, the Seyffarth family entered the social stratum schooled in the cultural values of German Idealism and the Classical world of Greek and Roman antiquity (*Bildungsbürger*). As a social class, *Bildungsbürger* held public office in the late stage of absolute monarchy. They were state administrators, attorneys, judges, professors, school directors and teachers, physicians, pharmacists, Protestant ministers, and engineers, and their status was primarily defined culturally, rather than socio- economically.

The seven children of Judge Seyffarth typified *Bildungsbürger*: Fritz (born 1872), became Chief Justice of the Supreme Court of Saxony; Lotte (born 1874), married the Director of the Imperial Postal Services, Berlin; Frieda (born 1876), married a regimental chief medical officer (WWI), later Professor of Medicine, Berlin; Paul-Erich (my grandfather, born 1877), became Regimental Chief Medical Officer (WWI), and Regional Medical Chief in the Hannover District; Martha (born 1879), became Senior Councillor of Studies (*Oberstudienrätin*), and married an architect in Königsberg; Ernst (born 1882), became an attorney in Berlin (killed in WWI, 1915); and Martin (born 1885), became a banker in Berlin (killed in WWI, 1914).

Early in the nineteenth century, *Bildungsbürger* typically supported the ideal of a liberal monarchy to replace the patchwork of hundreds of minor German principalities. However, by the 1870s, partly because of the failed liberal revolts against the European monarchies in 1848, and partly because of Prussia's success in unifying Germany in 1871 under the Hohenzollern crown, the *Bildungsbürger* class had become politically conservative. Their progressive liberalism gave way to a reactionary nationalism and socio-cultural elitism. Thomas Mann's famous novel Buddenbrooks (*Buddenbrooks: Verfall einer Familie*, 1901) powerfully chronicles the decline of the *Bildungsbürger* 1835-1870, in the Hanseatic city of Lübeck, an autonomous state within the newly founded German Empire.

Danzig (Polish Gdansk) and Thorn (Polish Toruń)

In 1907, my grandfather married his second cousin, Erna Deuser (born 1887), who came from a long line of master butchers,

master innkeepers, master fishermen, and fishpond owners in Danzig. The city has a fascinating history, alternating between German and Polish governments. The city was also populated by a third ethnic minority, the Kashubians, an indigenous West Slavic people that settled in the area some 1500 years ago. Even today, some 110,000 people still speak Kashubian at home.

The origin of ancient *urbs Gyddanyzc* is associated with the death of Christian missionary St. Adalbert in 997AD. The city lies at the point at which the river Weichsel (Polish Vistula), a crucial trading waterway, flows into the Baltic Sea. Seized by the Teutonic Knights, in 1308, the city was Polish as *Danczig* from 1466 until 1793, before being incorporated into Prussia as Danzig after the Napoleonic wars.

By 1910, most of the city's 170,000 residents spoke German. Lost to Germany by the Treaty of Versailles in 1918, Danzig became an independent city state (*Freistaat*). The city was annexed by Hitler in 1939 (thereby starting WWII), and became Polish again in 1945 as *Gdansk,* and its German population was expelled. Fisheries, ship-building, and the sea-borne trades have always been the hallmark of the city, no matter what the ethnicity of its population or its political governance.

Another city linked with my grandmother Deuser's family, even older than Danzig, is Thorn (Polish Toruń), settled during the Bronze Age by the Leusation people, whose languages and ethnic identity are unknown, but who left behind rich

Leusation cult wagon

Nobel Prize 1929

BUDDENBROOKS
THOMAS MANN

26

troves of artifacts, ceramics, grave goods, and cult objects. First mentioned as a town in 855 AD, Thorn was given its city charter in 1233 by the Teutonic Knights who built fortifications there, and for centuries the town was home to diverse ethnic groups and religious practices.

Also seated on the Weichsel River, the city from 1264 to 1411 was a leading trade center of the Hanseatic League, during which time it acquired the characteristic Gothic architecture still dominating its center today. (It was designated a World Heritage Site in 1997). Eventually part of the Polish kingdom, the town underwent the same seesaw of governance as Danzig, alternating between Polish, Prussian, and German sovereignty.

Paul Karl Seyffarth

In 1473, Nikolas Copernicus (known in Low German as Niclas Koppernigk), the founder of heliocentrism, was born in Thorn, then part of Royal Prussia. Copernicus was a child of the German-speaking patrician class. He used German in private, but Latin in his scientific writing and in commerce, and was also fluent in Polish.

My grandmother's father, Robert Deuser (1856-1924), born in Thorn, was a master butcher and owner of a meat plant. During his lifetime, the population of Thorn was sixty-seven per cent German, the rest Polish, many of them bilingual. The German majority was represented by liberal political associations supporting a united Germany on the foundation of the Revolution of 1848, while the Polish minority supported the national aspirations of Poland.

Robert Deuser married a woman from Danzig, and they had five children, four sons and a daughter. One of the sons became an art and book dealer, another a commercial artist, and a third an engineer. The fourth son died at birth, and the daughter married a banker, who was killed in WWI. The elder Deuser sold his business while still young, and took early retirement in Zoppot (Polish *Sopot*), a luxurious seaside resort in the Gulf of Danzig since the 16th century. Here my grandmother, Erna Deuser, grew into a young woman in fashionable ease. As I child, I remember her as a tall, thin and elegant woman, who funneled her esthetic sensibilities into beautiful clothes.

By contrast, my grandfather, Paul Karl Seyffarth, was a ruddy, vital and hard working young man. After finishing his medical degree, he got engaged, but in 1914 was drafted into the army, where he advanced to the rank of major as regimental physician. After the war, he settled into private practice. Of his two daughters, my mother, Ingeborg Gritta

"And If the World Were to Perish…"
Ingeborg Sehmsdorf-Seyffarth, 1946

Seyffarth was born in 1910, her sister Rose Margarete five years later. My mother inherited the artistic leanings of the Deuser family, but the robust physical stature of the Seyffarths. Rose was tall and elegant like her mother, and like her loved fashionable clothes. My mother once told me that she had wanted to study medicine, but that her parents thought it more suitable for a woman of her social class to attend art school, which she did. She enriched the lives of her children with beautifully illustrated children's books, and especially watercolors drawn from the life of Baron Münchhausen, the inventor of the tall tale. She sculpted and potted, worked in wood, straw, cloth, leather and many other materials. My favorite piece, which she carved shortly after the Allied bombing of Dresden in February, 1945, is a woodcut showing a man and his son standing by a tree they had just planted. Surrounding the scene, a quote from Martin Luther reads: "And if the world were to perish tomorrow, I would still plant my little apple tree today" (Sehmsdorf-Seyffarth, 1946).

Wehlau Horse Market during my Mother's Youth

Wehlau (Russian Znamensk)

After the disaster of WWI, my grandfather took a position as town physician in Wehlau on the Pregel River (Russian *Pregolya*), in Eastern Prussia. He held that position until appointed chief medical officer in the Hannover District, then a province of Prussia (1918-1946), now in the state of Lower Saxony.

Wehlau originated as an Old Prussian fort. The indigenous Prussians (Pruzzen) were a Baltic tribe that spoke an Indo-European language and worshipped native deities. As late as 1595, Lutheran pastor Caspar Henneberger, author of the first detailed map of Prussia, described a large oak tree sacred to the ancient Prussians. In the 1250s, the fort was seized by the Teutonic Knights who began colonizing the area with German settlers and gave the fort the name Wehlau. The town that sprang up around the fort received its civic charter in 1335. In 1349, the Knights established a Franciscan monastery in Wehlau in honor of Mary. In 1380 St. Jakob's Church was erected in the center of town. Wehlau became a hub for horse breeding, and by charter was allowed to hold annual fairs to buy and sell horses and cattle, as well as linen. My mother remembers as a child marveling at the hundreds of horses on display at the fair, and going ice skating on the fair grounds flooded by the Pregel River in winter.

In 1440, Wehlau became a founding member of the Prussian Confederation, a compact of nobles, clergy and cities formed in opposition to Teutonic rule, and in 1454, the region was incorporated into the kingdom of Poland. During the subsequent war, the Teutonic Knights retook the town and subsequently held it as a Polish fief. In 1519, the burghers of Wehlau were converted to Protestantism, and by the beginning of the twentieth century — when my grandfather lived there — the town had roughly 4,000 inhabitants, mostly German Lutherans. It was the seat of the regional courthouse, and boasted a school of higher education (*Gymnasium*).

At the end of WWI, when my grandfather opened a private practice in Wehlau, he settled in a large apartment across from St. Jacob's church at the center of the town. Besides the church, the town square held City Hall, major businesses, professional offices, and the homes of leading citizens. My grandfather's medical office and the family home occupied the entire second floor of a large and stately building. The family had a maid and a cook helping in the house. However, my grandfather was the only physician in Wehlau at the time, operating under difficult economic and material circumstances worsened by the harsh conditions imposed by the Treaty of Versailles. He brought a strong sense of the common good to his profession, an attitude I associate with the Prussian sense of civic duty.

In many ways, my grandfather personified the best of the Prussian virtues: He was austere, hard working, and honest. Although not a religious man, he was committed to service of his community rather than to his own economic advantage. He was also kind and forbearing. My mother remembered his spending endless days tending to patients in his office and about town, and the evenings poring over medical records. He served not only the townspeople, but also folks living in the rural area around Wehlau, reaching them by hired horse carriage in summer or sleigh in winter. When patients could not pay him in cash, he accepted whatever they could offer, some eggs, a chicken, or homemade bread. There was no hospital in town, and the physician had to make do with whatever he had at hand for surgical procedures or to deliver a

Ruin of St. Jakob's Church destroyed during WWII

Ingeborg Seyffarth, 1933

child. Once, when his daughter Rose suddenly came down with acute appendicitis, he operated on her on the kitchen table at home. Sanitary conditions were primitive. In Wehlau, as in most medieval towns until industrialization, waste water simply ran down the streets, draining as runoff into the local watershed.

With urbanization during the nineteenth century, the frequent outbreaks of water-born cholera and typhoid epidemics accompanied by high mortality rates, made sanitation urgent. In the 1840s, when much of Hamburg burned, vented flushing systems were developed to clean newly installed underground main line sewers. This design became the model for major cities in Europe and in America, with the earliest municipal sewage plants located in the Prussian North. In 1871, Danzig installed centralized sewage; in 1873, Berlin followed, decades earlier than industrialized cities like Heidelberg (1924), Munich (1925), not to mention smaller towns, like Wehlau.

My grandfather found respite from his strenuous work by drinking beer and playing cards at the local regulars' table (*Stammtisch*), friendly get-togethers at a reserved table in a cozy (*gemütlich*) local pub typically found in German towns and cities even today. He was an accomplished storyteller, delivering his tales in broad local dialect, in the sardonic and ribald style typical of Prussian humor.

Characteristically, the stories he told of war experiences did not

Woodcut, Heidlauken, Eastern Prussia, 1929. The text below reads: "Gustav, you got a girlfriend?" — "Yeah, sure" — "Well, who then?" "Don't know yet — depends who I run into."

dwell on the horrors he experienced as regimental physician, but on human foibles, often laced with sexual innuendo and rude descriptions of bodily processes. One of the stories I heard as an adult — he did not tell us these when we were children — recalled how at the Russian front he was relieving himself, crouching down in the bushes with his pants pulled down, when suddenly he spied

Bergenthal Manor, 1905-1910

a troupe of enemy soldiers reconnoitering the German lines. When they saw him, he motioned with his hand, and they threw down their weapons and followed him back to his camp. What a howler!

Another story told of an arrogant young lieutenant highly unpopular among the common soldiers because he took vain pride in his patent of nobility. One day in winter, when he put out his tall boots for his orderly to polish, the company passed them around and everyone pissed in them. The next morning, the boots were filled with frozen urine, much to the embarrassment of the officer when the trumpet blew for reveille. A third story told of my grandfather's coming into the surgical ward of his regiment early one morning to find a junior officer engaged in sexual intercourse with a nurse on the operating table. They couldn't come apart because of a severe case of *penis captivus*, and my grandfather had to apply anal massage to relieve the problem.

In Wehlau, the family's social circle mostly comprised the *Bildungsbürger* of the town, the pastor, the town lawyer, the apothecary, and school teachers. It also included the family of Robert Sarasin, whose noble manor farm *Bergenthal* lay right outside Wehlau. His daughter Jeanne (1906-2003) married Baron Wilhelm von Kuenheim, and she became a life-long friend of my mother's, when they both studied at the art academy in Königsberg in the 1920s. My mother's drawings, linoleum- and wood cuts from that period show great artistic talent. As a motif, she often chose the life of humble rural folks, whom she depicted with humor, sympathy, and a measure of upper class condescension.

In 1933, my mother's artistic career was cut short when she married my father, and over the next eleven years she bore seven children, the last three during the war. As an adult, I remember my mother expressing regret and some bitterness that her cousin, Susanne Seyffarth, had been allowed to study medicine, while she was not. But she also recognized that given social attitudes at the time, Susanne had to choose between a professional life and having a family; she never married. Late in his life, my father recalled that he met his future wife as a dance partner at his student fraternity at the University of Königsberg (K.-E, Sehmsdorf, 1996). Her own father frequented the dances as an "Old Man" (*alter Herr*), i.e. a lifetime member of the fraternity he had joined when studying medicine. Taking a teenage daughter to fraternity events functioned as a sort of "coming out" of young, marriageable women in the upper middle class.

I remember from my childhood that my parents owned a canvas folding kayak (*Klepperboat)*, and heard stories of how they had courted on unchaperoned river trips. As an adult, I learned from my mother's sister that while my father took advantage of these trips to be sexually intimate with my mother, he nevertheless judged her in keeping with the rigid puritanical moral code of the era. No doubt this moral double standard burdened the marriage of my parents, which ended in divorce in 1947 and had deleterious effects on the physical and emotional health of their children.

I was undernourished and physically weak during the war and remember being sent to *Bergenthal* Manor for summer vacations in the hope that I would gain some weight and my fragile health improve. I loved driving around in a horse carriage with the Baron overseeing the work in the fields. Most of the field workers were Polish and Russian prisoners of war replacing the Germans who had been drafted into the Army. The POWs were a friendly lot, and they let me ride on the backs of the plough horses, but at the end of the day "Auntie Kuenheim" had to pick the fleas out of the seat of my pants. She made magic for me by stirring an egg into sugar and the juice of a fresh orange until it filled a whole glass. The Kuenheims were famous for breeding horses, and I remember the Army coming to the manor to select the best animals for the war effort. The family abandoned *Bergenthal* Manor in 1945, when the Soviets overran the area.

The town of Wehlau was almost completely destroyed at the end of WWII, its German population expelled, and the town incorporated into the Kaliningrad Oblast, an exclave of the Soviet Union. In 2006, the Russian government stripped the town of its civic charter and demoted it to a rural settlement.

After the acrimonious divorce, the loss of our home near Dresden, and the separation of the family, Mother's existence became financially precarious. Her attempts after the war to earn a living as a commercial artist failed. She possessed neither the academic qualifications nor the economic means to study medicine. Instead, she trained in Kneipp therapy comprising naturopathic treatments through water, exercise, nutrition, and medicinal herbs. While naturopathic procedures were accepted by the general population, Kneipp hydrotherapy was not scientifically recognized until the 1980s and 1990s. However, my mother was able to make a modest living both as a therapist and as a Kneipp teacher. Later, she also was successful teaching German to foreign students attending private schools in Germany. At the end of her working life, she worked as a caretaker in retirement homes. During all these years, contact with her children remained sporadic, causing both her and the children much suffering.

Father's Family: Dauer, Züsedom & Podanin, Königsberg, Dresden, Heidenau, and After

From Sehmsdorf to Dauer

The first documented family member to carry the Sehmsdorf name was a blacksmith called Dietrich who settled in Dauer, Uckermark, during the second half of the seventeenth century. It is not known for certain when he was born or where, but apparently he emigrated from the village of **Sehmsdorf** in Holstein during the Thirty Years' War (1618-1648), and adopted the name of the village as his own. There is only one family bearing that name, and all its members, whether they lived, or today live, in Germany, Austria, Russia, North or South America, are related through their common descent from that one man.

What motivated Dietrich Sehmsdorf to uproot himself and move to the eastern province? Why did he take the name of the village as his family name? And why did he settle in Dauer?

In answering these questions much depends on what we can assume about his social status in his home village and in Dauer, and how the political, economic and cultural circumstances in either place shaped his mentality.

Dietrich's presumed ancestral home was a small agricultural settlement in Holstein, today a state in the Federal Republic of Germany, but at the time part of the Danish kingdom. Holstein's name comes from the *Holcetae* ("dwellers in the wood," from Northern Low Saxon *Hol(t)saten*; German: *Holzsassen*), a Saxon tribe mentioned in the eleventh century by bishop Adam of Bremen as living on the north bank of the Elbe, west of what today is Hamburg. Eastern Holstein was originally occupied by a Slavic tribe conquered in 1142 by Saxon duke Henry the Lion (*Heinrich der Löwe*) and settled with Saxon colonists, among them reputedly four

peasants at the place that came to be called Sehmsdorf (Manfred Sehmsdorf, 2020). The name is possibly toponymic, derived from Old High German *seim* (sticky, viscous fluid) + *dorf* (village), reflecting the production of honey in the region. In 1459 Holstein fell to the Danish Crown through dynastic union, and remained Danish until annexed by Prussia in 1864.

The farmers settled at Sehmsdorf were most likely serfs. They worked farmsteads allotted by noble landowners in exchange for payments and fixed labor services. The landowners had received title to their manors (*Rittergut)* in fief for military support of a feudal lord. In seventeenth century Denmark, there were about a thousand manors consisting of around eighty thousand farms, clustered in groups of up to twenty farms as villages. Perhaps a fourth of these manors were on Crown lands, the rest on lands that belonged to the Church or to the knights. A serf was bonded (*leibeigen*) to the land, meaning that he and his family couldn't leave or marry without the consent of the landowner who held juridical authority over his district. The German word for farm (*Hof*) derives from *Hufe* (hoof), meaning the measure of agricultural area allotted to tenant farmers based on soil fertility and what the farmer could plow with a horse in a day.

While most farmers were serfs, there were also freeholders, who either had inherited their land or bought their freedom. Craftsmen, however, were often free by virtue of their independent trade, even though they usually were poor and lived as cotters on or near a farm. As a blacksmith, Diedrich Sehmsdorf thus could have been a serf or a freeman. The distinction makes a difference in considering his motivation to emigrate.

At the time Dietrich left Holstein, the

Brandenburg margrave who initiated the German colonization of his eastern province, did not have domain over the village of Sehmsdorf and its inhabitants. However, the wife of King Christian IV of Denmark, who as Duke of Holstein held ownership of the lands where Sehmsdorf lay, was an aunt of the Brandenburg margrave. So it is entirely possible that the Margrave made use of his family connections to the feudal lord of Sehmsdorf to transfer Holstein serfs to Uckermark, among them perhaps the blacksmith Dietrich.

It is also possible, however, that as a free craftsman Dietrich emigrated to Prussia on his own initiative, perhaps because he was offered free ownership of land in Dauer. The village of Dauer, like the village of Sehmsdorf, had been devastated by war and pestilence, leaving it nearly depopulated. Like many emigrants before and after him, Dietrich may have responded to opportunities beckoning in a foreign place: access to land, economic opportunity, and the freedom to make a living on his own.

It is revealing to reflect on the cultural framework of the Thirty Years' War that may have had a direct bearing on why the blacksmith emigrated. The duration of the war coincides with the early Baroque period in Europe, a style that has been described as spanning simultaneous longing for escape (*Weltflucht*) and manic celebration of the world's transient beauty (*Weltsucht*). Religious poets and visionary writers, composers, painters, sculptors, and church architects created swelling, exuberant, at times gaudy and crude forms, colors, and language to voice despair over the degradation of a war-torn world, but also to celebrate the mystical beauty of nature (Trübner, 2011; Rogers, 1970).

Poet Christian von Hofmannswaldau (1616-1679), for example, castigated the treachery of deceitful enemies:

"Laß mich die Lust des Feindes nicht berücken,
Die Wermut oft mit Zucker überlegt,

Verwirrt ihn selbst im Garne seiner Tücken,
Daß der Betrug nach seinem Meister schlägt.
Laß mich bei guter Sach' ohn' alles Schrecken
stehen/ Und unverdienten Haß zu meiner Lust
vergehen."

(Don't let the enemy's lust ensnare me/Let the sugar-coated wormwood of his treachery/Confuse himself /Let his deceit strike back at its master/Let me stand by my good cause without trepidation/And undeserved hatred cease).

In contrast, Protestant mystic Jakob Böhme embraced transcendence to find release from temporal existence and strife:

Jakob Böhme, 1575-1624

"Wem Zeit ist wie Ewigkeit,
Und Ewigkeit wie die Zeit,
Der ist befreit
Von allem Streit."

(To whom time is like eternity/And eternity like time/He is set free/from all strife).

Böhme blazed an intellectual trail that would be followed by Spinoza (1632-1677), Goethe (1749-1832), and Rudolf Steiner (1861-1925) to provide new visions of the world's creation from divine Spirit. Böhme mirrors Gnostic, Kabbalistic, and Taoist concepts not common in Germany at the time. His idea of God as impersonal — the undifferentiated abyss (*Ungrund*) familiar from Eastern spirituality — was offensive to fellow Lutherans (Herd, 2003).

A major voice in contemporary culture was Heinrich Schütz, unquestionably the greatest composer of sacred music before Bach. In a series of liturgical compositions based on the Psalms of David, he wrote music "of archaic vehemence" (Steude, 1992). His widely performed liturgies mirrored the violence of war pitting kings against God's Anointed:

"Warum toben die Heiden/Und murren die Völker so vergeblich?/ Die Könige der Erde lehnen sich auf/Und die Herren halten Rat miteinander/Wider den Herrn und seinen Gesalbten: Lasset uns zerreißen unsere Bande/ und von uns werfen ihre Stricke" (Psalm 2: 1-3, Luther's translation).

(Why do the heathens rage/ And the people imagine a vain thing?/The kings of the earth set themselves against God's Anointed/And the rulers take counsel together/Saying, Let us break their bands asunder/ And cast away their cords from us (King James translation).

An illiterate blacksmith living in an isolated rural community would probably not have been exposed to the visual and verbal arts common in cultural centers during the Baroque period. However, in attending religious services, for instance, in the nearby town of Oldesloe, Dietrich would likely have heard the organ

music of Schütz, Froberger or Tunder, or sung the life-affirming hymns of Silesius Angelus, Fleming or Paul Gerhart (1607-1676), Lutheran minister and hymnodist:

"Das Haupt, die Füß und Hände/Sind froh, daß nun zu Ende/Die Arbeit kommen sei/ Herz, freu dich, du sollst werden/Vom Elende dieser Erden/Und von der Sünden Arbeit frei."

(Head, feet and hands/Are glad that now to an end/Their work has come/Oh, heart, rejoice, you're free/From the misery of this earth/And free of all the works of sin).

The blacksmith might also have witnessed theater troupes entertaining crowds at town markets with rude, topical plays reflecting the social realities of seemingly endless war.

The widespread depravities caused by the Thirty Years' War were also the sum and substance of the widely read picaresque novels of H. J. C. von Grimmelshausen, depicting realistically drawn characters against the background of a land degraded by violence, fear, hunger, and depopulation (Moore, 2013, 61ff). The son of an impoverished noble family, Grimmelshausen was pressed into service at age ten as a musketeer in the Imperial army. He taught himself to read and write, studied the law, and in 1639 escaped the army. He became a steward (*Arrendator*) to the Counts of Schauenburg, tasked with collecting taxes and fees from peasants and bringing defaulters to court. He held his position until 1660, when it was discovered that he had embezzled money from the family to buy land for himself. Grimmelshausen had begun writing in his soldier days and in 1669 published *Der abenteuerliche Simplicissimus*

Hans-Jakob C. von Grimmelshausen, 1621-76

Teutsch (The Adventures of Simplicius Simplicissimus), essentially the first novel in the German canon.

The author published a series of such novels under anagrams of his own name, except for the name of Michael Rechulin von Sehmsdorf, the putative author of *Das wunderbarliche Vogelsnest* (The Magical Bird's Nest, 1672). This satirical novel depicts a crude adventurer who poses as the Messiah to steal a wealthy Jew's daughter, and his money. The chosen pseudonym suggests that the author was familiar with the village from which Dietrich Sehmsdorf came, which he perhaps raided as a soldier. The magical bird's nest becomes the controlling metaphor for the cynical anti-hero whose invisibility permits him to dupe people at will — a fitting image of cultural instability during a time when illusion, gullibility, avarice and moral depravity became strategies for survival in an uncertain and cruel world (Negus, 1974, 124).

It is not far-fetched to speculate that what pulled the blacksmith into emigration was economic promise in a foreign land, but what pushed him were unbearable social conditions at home during the Thirty Years' War. In adopting the name of his native village as his family name, Dietrich followed an established custom. In most of Germany, the practice of using surnames was common by the 1500s. Before then, a person would be identified by adding the name of the father as a second name, combined with the suffix -son or -daughter, a practice still used in Iceland today. By 1812, Prussia required the adoption of permanent family names. Most commonly, people adopted a surname that reflected the man's trade, such as Smith, but a place could also supply a family with their name, as in the case of Dietrich, the blacksmith, who chose the name of his village.

From Dauer to Züsedom

Between the arrival of Dietrich Sehmsdorf in Dauer during the Thirty Years' War, and the purchase of the noble manor (*Rittergut*) Züsedom by his great-grandson, Daniel Sehmsdorf (1746-1824), the family achieved astounding upward social mobility. Over three generations, the descendants of the blacksmith became large landowners with all the privileges attached to that status, notably an absolute right to the land without any obligation to any landlord, sovereign, or government.

Medieval Church in Dauer, where Diedrich Sehmsdorf married and was buried, 2018

Today the former Züsedom manor is a small industrial village (*Ortschaft*) seven miles south of Pasewalk, an administrative center (*Amt*) of Vorpommern-Greifswald, rural district (*Landkreis*) of the German state of Mecklenburg-Vorpommern. The village lies in the flood plain of the Uecker River to the west, and the Randow River to the east, a distance of twenty-five miles from the Polish border.

Only the western quarter of Pomerania lies in Germany today. The remaining three provinces belong to Poland. Pomerania originally took its name from a West Slavic tribe that settled between the mouths of the Oder and Vistula Rivers after 650 AD. Its rulers became dukes holding the land in fief variously under the Teutonic Knights, the Holy Roman Empire, Poland, Denmark, and Sweden, until its western half was annexed by Brandenburg-Prussia as the result of the Great Northern War (1700-1721), half a century before Daniel Sehmsdorf settled on the manor owned by the Barons of Winterfeld. By that time, the population of Pomerania, decimated during several wars by as much as ninety percent, had again risen to the levels preceding the Thirty Years War.

Czusdom Manor was first mentioned in a document in 1367. In 1650, the manor came to the Electress of Brandenburg, then to the Barons von Oldenvliet, von Lindstedt, and von Winterfeld. After Daniel Sehmsdorf owned it for four decades (1802-1842), it was briefly held by Dr. Menz and then sold to the Counts von Arnim who lived there until it was overrun by the Soviets in 1945. In 1952, the village of Züsedom was assigned to the Pasewalk district in the Neubrandenburg district; in 2012, the community was incorporated into Rollwitz (Arnim, 2010).

After Dietrich Sehmsdorf had arrived in Dauer, he married the daughter of another blacksmith who is described in the genealogical record as a *Hofmann*, that is, a small-holder of undefined tenancy (Sedelmayer, 2018). He might have been a serf, or someone who rented the farm or managed it on behalf of a landlord. His son, Joachim Samuel Sehmsdorf (1670-1748), however, became an arrendator who leased fixed assets, such as a land holding or the right to collect rent on behalf of a landlord or taxes on behalf of the Crown. Historically, an arrendator was allowed to keep a portion of the money in exchange for this service. The practice, also referred to as rent-revenue farming, was extremely lucrative and often led to fiscal abuse. This is not to say that Joachim Samuel Sehmsdorf abused his lease, but it

appears that the office he held for many years laid the foundation for the family's wealth. It also means that while the blacksmith Dietrich Sehmsdorf most likely was illiterate, his son Joachim must have had the necessary schooling to qualify for the arrendator's position: to read and write and do the necessary math to keep accounts.

This momentous social shift was made possible by school reforms introduced in 1763 by Friedrich the Great, requiring all girls and boys from the age of five to thirteen or fourteen to attend municipally-funded kindergartens and schools (Horn, 2003). The first teacher seminar was founded in 1748, establishing teaching as a profession, and resulting in a system of public education internationally admired for its reducing illiteracy. The Prussian educational model was eventually emulated throughout Germany and in other countries, including Japan and the United States, which established compulsory public education a century later. Besides academic subjects, the schools served to instill the Prussian virtues of orderliness, punctuality, thrift, hard work, endurance, restraint, dependability, a sense of duty, and honesty, officially promoted by the Crown since the rule of Friedrich the Great's father.

Friedrich Samuel Sehmsdorf (1708-1775) followed in the footsteps of his father to become an arrendator in service of the Crown. He also became steward of several manors on Crown land or in private hands. For example, he managed the Ziemkendorf Manor (owned by the Counts of Eickstedt between 1325 until the outbreak of WWII). My father, who visited the Ziemkendorf Manor in the 1980s, described it as a rather modest house, in contrast to the manor house on Züsedom which he characterized as "palatial" (K.-E. Sehmsdorf, 1996).

In 1802, Züsedom manor was purchased by Daniel Johann Friedrich Sehmsdorf (1746-1824), the son of Friedrich Samuel. Daniel grew up on the manor farms managed by his father and attended the public schools in nearby towns. Whether he received higher education is not known, but he was clearly a man of talent and ambition. By 1774 Daniel became the leaseholder of Züsedom Manor then owned by Baron Friedrich von Winterfeldt. In 1792 Daniel made a formal survey (*Bonitierung*) of Züsedom Manor to establish its total size at 4,208 acres (Grude, 1981), and to document the suitability of the sandy loam soils and temperate climate (average annual temperature 54 degrees Fahrenheit and 22 inches of rain) to produce grains and potatoes, a crop first introduced to Europe by Friedrich the Great in 1741 (Sedelmayer, 2018).

In 1796, Daniel loaned the Baron the sum of 2,000 *Reichsthaler Courant* (a 1-ounce silver coin used in the Holy Roman Empire since 1524) at four per cent interest. In 1799, the Baron, by now bankrupted by the expense of attending the royal court in Berlin as required of an officer, petitioned the King for permission to sell the allodial estate — i.e. land owned by occupancy and defense on behalf of the sovereign — to a non-noble. The request was granted by cabinet order two years later, a year after the Baron's death. The Baron's son, Heinrich von Winterfeld, royal tax and rent collector (*Königlicher Kriegs- und Domänenrat*), inherited Züsedom, and in 1800 he borrowed another 8,000 *Reichsthaler* from his leaseholder. In 1802 the younger Winterfeld cured the family's debts by selling the manor to Daniel Sehmsdorf for the money owed, plus an additional 52,000 *Reichsthaler* and 20,000 *Friedrich d'or* (a gold coin worth 5 silver *Thalers*).

Frederik d'or, 1774

Several matters make the sale of Züsedom to Daniel Sehmsdorf remarkable. One is the sale of a noble manor (*Rittergut*) to a commoner. A second is the great monetary value of the transaction, and the underlying question of how the buyer raised that much money. A third concerns the labor requirements of such a large agricultural enterprise, and how laborers were compensated for their work in an era transitioning from medieval serfdom (Berghaus, 1868).

At the time Daniel Sehmsdorf acquired Züsedom as his own property, the baronial owner had to get special permission from the Crown for a variance to Prussian law linking the right of land ownership to a patent of nobility (Brooks, 2019, Schiller, 2003). The review process at the highest level took two years to complete (1899-1801). By taking ownership of a *Rittergut*, Daniel acquired legal rights traditionally reserved for the nobility. The most important of these were the rights to independent jurisdiction (*Patrimonial-Gerichtsbarkeit*), police authority, and church and school patronage.

As manor owner, Daniel was also favored by district and municipal regulations in regard to hunting rights, taxes, and the right to settle inheritance within a particular social group, usually the family. After Prussia's defeat at the hands of Napoleon, the Stein-Hardenberg Reforms of 1806-1807 uncoupled these rights legally from noble privilege (Scheel, 1966-1968). In turn, the reforms permitted nobles to pursue professions. This change was made necessary by industrialization and the shift of capital from land ownership to the trades and manufacturing centered in towns and cities. In practice, however, the linkage between land ownership and legal privileges continued at least until 1849, when the Frankfurt National Assembly enshrined the principle of universal equality of all citizens in a proposed national constitution to suspend all class privileges and basically turn manorial lords into mere landowners (Carr 1979, 46–48; Frotscher, 2005).

At the same time, the traditional linkage between land ownership and nobility continued to motivate bourgeois manor owners to seek nobilitation by virtue of land ownership. Even if certain material privileges were no longer founded in law, holders of patents of nobility wished to protect the symbolic capital of the family name in a society where the nobility continued to play a prominent role. To secure a title of nobility cleared the path to upward social mobility through privileged access to higher education, membership in certain foundations and on important boards, and accelerated advancement in military rank. The Stein-Hardenberg Reforms envisioned a new "knighthood" continuing linkage of nobility to land ownership, on the assumption that such linkage gave nobles the necessary independence and concomitant sense of responsibility. Therefore the aim was to raise qualified commoners to noble rank so that they could take their rightful place in advanced positions in state administration, the military, the sciences and the arts. But ownership of land always remained an indispensable prerequisite. Nobility was seen as a natural and necessary component of the monarchical system (Kucera, 2012).

There is no documentation to show that the Sehmsdorf family ever sought formal nobilitation, but the idea of "noblesse oblige" linked to land ownership continued to inform family tradition until quite recently. The fact that several generations of the family owned manor farms, or managed them on behalf of noble families such as the Counts of Schwerin-Schwarzenfeld, left a deep imprint on family traditions of expected virtues, social obligation, achievement, and privilege, even long after the descendants of the Züsedom gentry left behind farming as their principal livelihood.

Marion Sehmsdorf, wife of missionary pastor Georg Sehmsdorf (my father's oldest brother), in one of her short stories embodied the social code of "noblesse oblige" in the fictional character of Baron von Rüdersdorf. The story shows the personal price paid for absolute commitment to a transpersonal cultural norm. The baron saw the family's patent of nobility not as a seal of privilege, but of responsibility. His austere idealism made him a stranger to his family and children, but also "the irrefutable, absolute norm of their own thinking and acting," which gave them a sense of safety in an unsafe world (Marion Sehmsdorf, 1951, 12).

As the second eldest son, my great-grandfather could not inherit Podanin Manor, and so he became a grain wholesaler instead. His son, my grandfather, became a scholar and teacher; my father, a lawyer. But his sister, Lotte, in her memoir described the family as "rooted in agriculture." Like Thomas Jefferson, she saw land ownership as the foundation of civic virtue and social obligation. However, for Jefferson, the yeoman farmer's economic independence enabled him to vote his conscience in support of the civic freedoms guaranteed by the American Constitution. By contrast, the landed nobility of Prussia, also referred to as "Junkers" (from Middle High German *Juncherre*, meaning "young noblemen"), gave their loyalty to the absolute Hohenzollern monarchy. The Junkers owned most of the arable land in Prussia held in great estates worked by tenants and peasants who had few rights (Carsten, 1989).

The orientation of the landowning classes to the Crown also extended to the family structure patterned on the royal model. As the king who promulgated himself as *pater patriae* (*Landesvater*), so the male head of the household as *pater familias* (*Familienvater*) exercised legal authority over his wife and children in enforcing the virtues promoted by the Crown. On both levels of society paternalistic authority was linked to the will of God. The shadow side of this authority manifested whenever the father figure was lacking in kindness and empathy, and instead ruled in anger. The Teutonic Knights who had been sworn to the love of Christ, instead had violently suppressed the recalcitrant Old Prussians who refused to accept baptism. Likewise the strict and austere Soldier King, while a loyal husband, caused his wife and son to fear his violent temper that would flare into physical abuse. Friedrich the Great did not indulge in cruel rages as his father had, but he enforced his sense of justice by occasionally caning public servants who failed in their duties. Many a Prussian father beat his disobedient children to bend them to a

Manor Workers and Inspector, 18th-19th century Prussia

behavioral code authorized by the example of the divine right ruler, and often did so in uncontrolled, self-indulgent rage.

There are intimations in my family history that Daniel Sehmsdorf followed this pattern. After the deaths of his first two wives, who had borne him four daughters and two sons, he sired two more children with his housekeeper, Marie Zachert (1771-1855), the daughter of a local shoemaker. She apparently refused to marry Daniel from fear of his cantankerous personality and violent outbursts (K.-E. Sehmsdorf, 1996). After the two elder sons died, one from tuberculosis, the other during the Napoleonic wars, leaving Daniel without a male heir, he legitimized the two children born out of wedlock, a daughter named Auguste (born 1802) and a son named Julius (born 1811), my great-great-grandfather (Werner Grude, 1979).

A second compelling question regarding the purchase of Züsedom concerns the market value of the manor, and how Daniel was able to finance its acquisition. Unfortunately, the documents that might have thrown a direct light on this question have been lost. However, we have indirect evidence for what the property might have been worth and the monetary value of what the buyer actually paid for it.

In 1802 Daniel settled the bankruptcy claims against Züsedom manor by paying the Winterfeld family the equivalent of 162,000 Silver Thalers. At the time, the purchasing power of 1 Silver Thaler was roughly the same a 1 Silver Dollar. Given an average inflation rate of the Dollar of 1.40% per year between 1800 and today (Official Data 2023), producing a cumulative price increase of 2,112.71 percent, the price paid for the manor would amount to the equivalent of $3,585,060 today — about a fifth of what four thousand acres of cropland are currently worth in the U.S. — not counting the manor house and other infrastructure (Deutsche Bundesbank, 2023).

So it would seem that Daniel Sehmsdorf bought Züsedom at a huge bargain. But that still leaves unanswered how he managed to accumulate enough wealth to finance the purchase. Had three generations of arrendators collecting rents and taxes for noble landlords accumulated enough set-asides by honest means to rise from the ranks of landless peasants to those of privileged owners of a huge estate? Had Daniel over thirty years as leasehold-manager of Züsedom earned enough profit to cure the Baron's bankruptcy? Did his two first wives, both of whom were daughters of arrendators and leasehold farmers, bring substantial dowries when they married Daniel?

Or did he have to encumber the manor with further debts? The answers to these questions were perhaps found among the family papers my grandfather kept in a safe in Königsberg; but they were lost in the Russian bombings of 1945 (K.-E. Sehmsdorf, 1996).

A third question concerns how such an huge agricultural enterprise was actually managed, and who did the work? Who did the ploughing and harrowing, manuring, and sowing? Who put the harvest in the barn for threshing or storage, or take it to market? By 1800, agrarian Prussia had become the world's most productive agricultural region (Henning, 1978). But it had done so mostly on the backs of an enserfed peasantry deprived of liberty and personal rights, over whom manorial owners exercised nearly complete control. Much of this changed between the time when Daniel Sehmsdorf became leaseholder of Züsedom in 1771 and when he purchased the manor three decades later.

The institution of serfdom (*Leibeigenschaft)* has ancient roots (Zeuske, 2019). The rural populations (*helos*) surrounding Sparta, for example, were tied to the land they worked to support urban elites. Similarly, in 332 AD Roman emperor Constantine issued legislation that bound peasants (*coloni)* to the land and required them to provide agricultural labor. After the break-up of the Carolingian empire in the tenth century, powerful feudal lords in Northern Europe adopted serfdom, forcing peasants to feed them without pay, while holding them down legally and economically. The term "serf" comes from Latin *servus* (slave), in medieval England often called "villeins" or villagers, meaning feudal tenants entirely subject to a lord or a manor to whom they paid dues and services in return for land they could work to support themselves. But by 1400, with the rise of powerful monarchs and

Serfs paying dues.
Medieval woodcut (anon.)

towns, servitude to the nobility became rare, and disappeared by the sixteenth century in much of Western Europe. The increasing use of money made farming by serfs less profitable. Paid labor proved more efficient because hired workers tended to be better skilled, and motivated.

In England, Elizabeth I freed the last remaining serfs in 1574. In France, serfdom *de facto* ended by the fifteenth century, but was not formally abolished until 1789 in the aftermath of the French Revolution. During the violent overthrow of both the Capetian dynasty and the nobility, feudal rights were abolished. The jurisdiction of the manorial courts was canceled, the rights of landlords to impose annual fees eliminated, and any peasants still bound to the land were freed. However, ownership of the land remained in the hands of the wealthy landlords, who continued collecting rents and enforcing tenant contracts.

In Eastern Europe, the Teutonic Knights in the early thirteenthth century had enserfed the Old Prussians who refused to submit to Christianization. By contrast, landlords in the Polish-Lithuanian Commonwealth created peasant-friendly environments to attract eastward migration of agricultural workers. However, when the Bubonic Plague decimated populations causing severe labor shortages in the East, the nobles again began to bind the remaining peasantry to their land. The repressive Prussian Ordinances of 1525 limited serfs' legal and economic rights once more.

In contrast to the violence of the French Revolution, German emancipation of the serfs began peacefully in the 1770s, and was gradually completed over the next fifty years. In 1779, the Schleswig nobility voluntarily freed the peasants in their state. Prussian nobles, who for decades had been able to amass huge estates by evicting peasants without compensation, resisted initially. But in 1801, the Calvinist rulers of

Upper left: Züsedom Manor; upper right: Church, School, Farm Buildings; lower right: Farm Smithy and Dairy; lower left: Village Inn (19th-century postcard)

Prussia abolished serfdom by royal edict, with other German states following Prussia's example by 1815.

Royal protection for the peasants (*königlicher Bauernschutz*) was shaped by the Calvinist doctrine that living the Christian virtues was evidence of divine election. Also influential was the Enlightenment philosophy embodied in Kant's *Critiques* (1781-1790), arguing that the dignity — and immortality — of man lay in his freedom to obey the divine moral law in his heart. The *October Edicts* of 1807 granted the peasants ownership of half or two-thirds of the lands they had been working, both on Crown lands and noble estates, with the manorial owners retaining ownership of the balance of the land. The peasants no longer had to provide unpaid labor or annual dues to the lord. A peasant could now sell his land and move away, or buy his neighbor's land. As the result of this royal initiative, a large class of small farmers emerged that was loyal to the Crown. However, for most peasants, until well into the twentieth century, traditional life and custom continued unchanged, including the old habit of deferring to the paternalistic authority of the nobility (Cord, 2007).

East of the Elbe River, the "Junkers" continued to maintain large estates and monopolize political power. The division of the Commons (*Gemeinheiten*) into private parcels created a more efficient market-oriented rural economy, increasing productivity and stimulating population growth. However, as wealthier peasants obtained more of former manor land, poorer rural workers were left without any land and reduced to employment at low wages. Many left for the cities or emigrated to America. In *Das Kapital* (1867), Karl Marx claimed that the transformation of feudal serfdom into a system of private property and free labor was "nothing else than the historical process of divorcing the producer from the means of production." He held that land owners profited by stealing the value of the workers' labor and creating a new class of dispossessed wage earners.

Field Stone Granary on Züsedom Manor, 2018

He argued further that both wage earners and land owners operating on a commercial basis were spiritually "alienated" from the land and from their work.

Daniel Sehmsdorf's tenure on Züsedom over half a century spans the transition from serfdom to peasant emancipation. During the first three decades of management of the manor he would have forced serfs to work without compensation. During the last two decades he employed nominally free laborers at contractual wages.

A Prussian *Hufe* (from *Hof*, meaning farm) measured about 40 acres (after 1815, 18.9 acres), representing the amount of land needed for a single subsistence household. By that standard, managing Züsedom's four thousand acres would have required a hundred or more households of ploughmen, harvesters, cattlemen, shepherds, dairy workers, bakers, harness- and shoemakers, and many other craftspeople and servants, not to mention the numerous staff needed to run the manor household.

Züsedom Chapel, 2018

The farm households were settled on low-lying land adjacent to the manor house, in semi-circle or horse-shoe clusters (*Rundlinge*) of seven to twenty farmsteads comprising the village of

Züsedom. The seven hundred-year old field-stone chapel and the burial grounds (where Daniel was laid to rest— Wilfried Grude, 1981) were established closer to the manor house, on ground higher than the village water table. Destroyed by the Russian army in 1945, the chapel was rebuilt in 1966.

The socio-economic hierarchy of Züsedom was topped by the manor owner (*Gutsbesitzer*), which is the term used after 1850 for a large estate farmer owning at least 500 acres. "Lord of the Manor" (*Rittergutsbesitzer*) was the title reserved for the owner of large medieval estate farms originally owned by nobility.

Until 1807, most of the agricultural workers on Züsedom Manor were serfs who could not leave the land without the landowner's consent. As feudal tenants, they paid dues and several days of weekly labor in return for a small plot of land on which to support their own families. Serfs were entitled to protection and justice under manorial jurisdiction. They were also entitled to seeds for their own crops, and for economic support in case of crop failure or natural disaster. Given the power of the manor lord, it was up to him how lenient he was in enforcing his privileges, and how generous in supplying the serfs' needs. In contrast to a notorious manor lord in Schleswig-Holstein reported to kick and whip the last serf reporting to work on any given morning, we can only hope that Daniel Sehmsdorf — in spite of his cantankerous reputation — treated his workers with more kindness and forbearance.

We can distinguish different kinds of farm workers by their occupational designations. The largest group were the landless laborers (*Instleute*) who worked in the fields, stables, workshops, and in the manor house

(Haxthausen, 1839). Field workers usually had to provide an additional helper, commonly an unmarried son or daughter (*Scharwerker*). All adult members of serf families were required to provide labor in exchange for daily in-kind compensation (*Deputat, Tagelohn*), such as grain, potatoes, vegetables, clothing, housing as needed, and small cash payments. Younger family members were employed as apprentices (*Lehrling*). Cooks, maids, servants, and coachmen attached to the manor house were quartered there (*Einlieger*), housed in shacks in the village (*Kätner*), or in rooms rented in somebody else's house (*Beilieger*). Serfs who managed a small farm on land owned by the manor (*Hofland*) were required to work as teamsters (*Spannführer*), bringing their own teams of usually four horses (*Gespann*). Non-field workers (*Arbeitsmann*), such as smiths, rope and harness makers, shoemakers, spinners, dairy workers, and bakers lived in rooms attached to workshops on the manor.

Landless workers who did not own a house or other assets, had no voice in community meetings. The village community also featured tenant store owners (*Hakenbüdner* or *Höker*), who displayed merchandise on hooks from the walls and ceilings of their shops, pub owners (*Schankwirt*), and pharmacists who dispensed medicines, first aid, and dental care — all of these establishments owned and licensed by the landlord.

Workers assigned to tasks of long term responsibility to the manor enjoyed elevated socio-economic status. The designated farm manager (*Ökonom* or *Verwalter*) managed daily work schedules; the bookkeeper (*Rendant*) kept daily accounts; the granary manager (*Kämmerer*) controlled the grain storage and distributed daily rations to workers and teamsters for their horses; and the housekeeper (*Wirtschafter/ -in*) managed the domestic staff and kept supplies under lock and key. This was the occupation of Marie Zachert (1771-1855) who was hired by Daniel Sehmsdorf as his housekeeper in 1801, and subsequently bore him two children, including his only surviving heir.

Besides the serfs, in most agricultural communities there were a limited number of free yeoman farmers (*Bauern*) who owned their land outright by inheritance or purchase (*Bauernland*). There were also tenant farmers (*Pächter*), who leased the land from the manor, but did not have to provide labor. Sometimes a collective group of farmers (*Nachbarschaft*) would together farm acreage leased from a landlord. The free yeoman farmers dominated the village socio-economically. From their ranks the arrendators (from vulgate Latin *arenda*, meaning "lease fee") were recruited and licensed to collect rents, taxes, custom duties and fees from serfs and from leaseholders of mills, inns, breweries and distilleries on behalf of landlords and governments. From the sixteenth to the eighteenth centuries, the system was in wide use in Portugal, Spain, and Prussia, and in Russia well into the nineteenth century. Arrendators were allowed to keep a portion of the money in exchange for this service. The fiscal practice often led to corruption, partly because the arrendators also acted as bailiffs bringing serfs and leaseholders to court if they failed to pay. Many Prussian manor farms were managed by arrendators on behalf of absentee landlords. Züsedom manor was managed for three decades by Daniel Sehmsdorf in his dual role as leaseholder and arrendator.

Most large estates grew rye, wheat, potatoes (introduced by Friedrich the Great in 1744), vegetables, and meadow hay for livestock feed. Rye was the most important cultivated crop in eighteenth to nineteenth-century Prussia, with wheat accounting for less than five percent of total grain production. Animal production typically included horses, oxen and dairy animals, pigs and poultry for home use and for market. Targeted soil improvement practices were part of building farm capital. Expanding urban demands around the turn of the nineteenth century increased the profitability of high-yielding intensive farming systems and grassland farming. When it came to land taxes (up to thirty percent of Prussian state income), manor farms were given preferential treatment.

Podanín

When Daniel Sehmsdorf died in 1824, his only living son and heir, Julius Sehmsdorf (1811-1900), was thirteen years old, too young to manage the manor. Züsedom was sold to Dr. Mentz, who in 1842 resold the manor to the Counts von Arnim. The Arnim family managed the manor until it was overrun by the Russians in 1945. Because the mother of Julius, Marie Zachert, had never married his father, she could neither inherit nor manage the manor herself (E. Sehmsdorf, 1935), and Züsedom

Palais Hardenberg: Seat of House of Representatives, Lower House of the Prussian Parliament, 1850-1918

passed out of the Sehmsdorf family.

We do not know where and under what circumstances Julius was raised after leaving Züsedom, but he must have attended good schools. A granddaughter of Julius (Margarethe Köllner, née Sehmsdorf) writes in her family chronicle that Julius spoke fluent French and was well versed in Latin, studied law and started a legal career at the court of appeals (*Auskalkulator*). In 1837 he married Adolfine Albrecht, who died a year later after giving birth to a daughter, Marie Elisabeth. In 1839, he married Mathilde Vanselow, who bore him six children and raised the firstborn as her own. The couple also had stillborn twins, baptized Adolf and Adolfinchen after Julius' first wife. Adolfine apparently remained the love of his

life ("*mein einziges Glück*"), which occasionally filled the children of his second marriage with indignation when in his dotage Julius spoke of his first wife as if she were still living (Walter, 1935).

For health reasons (apparently he suffered from a weak heart), Julius found that a lawyer's career tying him to a desk was not a good choice, and he decided to return to his agricultural roots. In 1840 he leased a manor farm at Böthin (Polish *Bytyń*) near Tütz (Polish *Tuczno*), a municipality today located in the province (*Voivodeship*) of Polish West Pomerania. He managed Böthin Manor for just a year. In 1841, he bought the sixteen hundred-acre Podanin Manor in Posen Province (Polish *Poznan*). There he lived until 1878, when he handed Podanin over to his son Otto and retired to nearby Bromberg (Köllner, 1924).

Julius purchased Podanin Manor as a "free mayoral farm" (*Freischulzenhof*), meaning that it was tax-free because its owner was appointed *ex officio* deputy mayor (*Schulze, Amtmann*), which office remained attached to the manor in perpetuity.

As a large landowner, Julius was expected to be involved in local, state, and even national politics. In response to the Revolutions of 1848, King Friedrich Wilhelm IV authorized primaries for electing a Parliament for the Kingdom of Prussia (*Preußischer Landtag*). These primaries took place at the same time electors were chosen for the German National Assembly in Frankfurt charged with writing a German Constitution. In 1948, Julius attended the Frankfurt assembly representing Posen and argued against inclusion of the Polish parts of the district in a unified Germany (K-E. Sehmsdorf, 1980).

By installing the Prussian Parliament, the King hoped to control the revolution and prevent the adoption of a state constitution to end the absolute monarchy. The electoral law provided equal and indirect suffrage for all men over the age of twenty-four not on poor relief. It was the broadest electoral franchise of all German

Julius Sehmsdorf and Family at his golden wedding on Podanin Manor, 1988

states at the time. The Prussian Parliament consisted mostly of public servants and conservative artisans, farmers and large landowners, while the Frankfurt National Assembly included large numbers of liberal academics and writers.

From 1868-1870, Julius Sehmsdorf served as representative from Posen County to the Lower House of the Prussian Parliament (*Abgeordnetenhaus*) Politically, he was aligned with the National Liberal faction around Wilhelm Grabow (Kiepert, 13-15). Grabow had written the original electoral law granting male suffrage and had fought for the establishment of a constitutional monarchy. King Friedrich-Wilhelm IV had fled to England during the uprisings against the monarchy in 1848. When he returned, he had appointed Otto von Bismarck, who was firmly committed to divine right rule, prime minister of Prussia. Bismarck

had passed legislation to suppress socialist-liberal impulses against the absolute monarchy. When the National Assembly in Frankfurt had adopted a federal constitution and offered the office of hereditary German emperor to Friedrich-Wilhelm, the King had refused to accept the crown from the hands of a popularly elected assembly. This ended the efforts to unify Germany by peaceful means. Instead Bismarck's policy of guarding the absolute power of the Hohenzollern monarchy prevailed. In 1862 he declared to the Prussian House of Representatives: "The position of Prussia in Germany will not be determined by its Liberalism but by its power ... Not through speeches and majority decisions will the great questions of the day be decided—but by "iron and blood" (Petersdorff, 1924-1935, 139-40).

Julius Sehmsdorf was aligned with the Liberal faction favoring a constitutional monarchy.

However, according to an anecdote my father learned from his own father, Bismarck is supposed to have sneered that the most conservative legislator actually was not seated among his own Conservatives, but among the National Liberals, namely "Old Sehmsdorf" (*der Alte Sehmsdorf*), who showed his conservatism by still wearing pants with a buttoned flap in the seat instead of in front, as in modern fashion (K.-E. Sehmsdorf, 1996). Bismarck's rude remark astutely deflected criticism of his own reactionary policies by deliberately confusing cultural conservatism with the political sort represented by his own support for the absolute monarchy.

As elected district representative, Julius often stood in for the district administrator (*Landrat*), for instance, during the Polish uprisings in Prussia in 1848 (Wuttke, 237-259). This is a painful chapter in Prussia's history in the partition of Poland, and its aftermath for the people in the Posen area. After the third and final partition of Poland, Friedrich the Great had settled some fifty-eight thousand German families in the new Prussian territories.

Langenscheidt's French-German Encyclopedia, 1964

But by 1848 more than seventy percent of the population remained Polish, and German was still the minority language. However, the Poles were systematically excluded from state administration, the educational system, and land ownership. The 1848 social revolutions strengthened Polish aspirations to self-governance. In response, German craftsmen, traders and recent settlers formed paramilitary groups to prevent Poles from organizing. By late April about eight thousand Germans in the Nestle (Polish *Noteć*) district organized in paramilitary units and another six thousand around the towns of Meseritz (Polish *Międzyrzecz*) and Neutomischel (Polish *Nowy Tomyśl*). As district administrator Julius Sehmsdorf played a "very energetic" (*sehr energische*) role in organizing the German reaction, but no specifics of his leadership have been documented (Köllner, 1924).

Privately, Julius Sehmsdorf was a man with a playful sense of humor, a lover of good cigars and rich food and drink. He indulged in telling funny anecdotes about mentally unstable King Wilhelm IV (replaced in 1857 by his brother as regent, the future Emperor Wilhelm I). Julius engaged a capable farm manager, and the manor thrived especially during the Crimean War (1853-1856), which forced Russia to buy great quantities of Prussian grain at inflated prices — leaving Julius free to spend time with his beloved linguistic studies. He collaborated with pioneering etymologist August F. Pott (1802-1887) to produce the French-German encyclopedia *Sachs-Villatte* still published by Langenscheidt today (J. Sehmsdorf, 1876). His grandchildren recalled Julius taking walks with his pockets stuffed with sheafs of vocabularies he was investigating. Without warning, he would stop to pull a paper from his pocket and race back home to note something he had suddenly remembered. His love of learning was also manifested in his longterm support of a nephew who studied theology, and their copious correspondence in Latin. The nephew eventually became a noted scholar of ancient history and Royal Curator for Antiquities in Pomerania (Köllner, 1924; Biewer 2000; Aldermann, 2000).

Podanin Manor was a hospitable house, with an active social life, and much visiting back and forth between large families, storytelling, and dancing. The extended family would begin their holidays on the manor. On the first days of Easter or Christmas, for example, relatives and friends would drive or sled out to Podanin with their children in the morning and stay for the day until supper.

But while his wife was unfailingly generous and kind, Julius' grandchildren were afraid of him because of an inherited choleric temper. By cultural habit, many a Prussian father from the King on down permitted himself to fly off the handle . Uncontrolled anger was justified as frankness (*Redlichkeit*), or straightforwardness (*Geradlinigkeit*), both acknowledged Prussian virtues. To his credit, Julius was usually sorry for his outbursts, and he often said, "Now I've become so violent again" (*nun bin ich doch wieder so heftig geworden*), but apparently never learned to control his temper (Köllner, 1924).

Julius died in his 90th year, cigar in hand. He was such a strong and colorful personality that whoever knew him, did not soon forget him. In 1888, twelve years before his death, Julius and his wife celebrated their golden wedding which brought together most of the extended family for the last time.

In the wedding photo, Julius (second row from bottom) is shown wearing an embroidered smoking cap, with his beloved granddaughter, Käthe (my grandfather's sister) leaning on his knee, and his wife, Mathilde (1814-1892) seated to his right.

His son Ernst (fifth row from bottom, center), was an officer in the Army Reserves, and a passionate hunter. As the eldest, he was intended to inherit Podanin Manor. However, he suffered a serious accident working on his own manor (Johannesburg near Krone at the Brahe River), and relinquished Podanin to his brother Otto (1843-1901). After giving up farming, Ernst (1840-1906) pursued a career in public administration, and became mayor, county commissioner, and police superintendent for the district of Kolmar.

Otto (second left, fourth row from bottom) and his wife Olga (1859-1944) had two sons. Fritz became a magistrate in Berlin, and Hans a major general in the Prussian infantry. Neither of them was interested in farming, leaving management of the manor to their mother, who eventually sold it around 1907, meaning that this manor, too, passed out of the family. Georg (1846-1901), the third son (fourth row from bottom, right) established a grain wholesale company in Berlin. He married his distant cousin Margarethe (Meta) Ring (1848-1980), whom he had met when she

visited Podanin Manor as a girl. Their son Erich (1875-1940) was my grandfather, and his sister Käthe (1878-1951) the favorite aunt in my family.

Hugo (third row from bottom, left), the fourth son, was leaseholder of the five thousand-acre Sartowitz Manor in Graudenz, which belonged to the Counts of Schwerin-Schwanenfeld.

Emil (top row, right), the fifth son, was director of a large brewery in Odessa, Ukraine, and married to a Russian woman (Trinitschka, third row from bottom, right). He died young from cancer, leaving behind a son (Alexander, bottom row, left) who became a physician, and a daughter (Ernestine, standing between Julius and Mathilde). She became a teacher, but is believed to have perished during the Russian Revolution. Not shown in the picture is a sixth son, Friedrich, who emigrated to America and died young in New York City. His daughter Susanna returned to Germany impoverished and in poor health and was raised by her grandparents. She eventually married her cousin Herman Walter (top row, second from right) and died in Hamburg, leaving no children. A second daughter of Friedrich's stayed in America, but nothing is known of her own life or of that of her mother.

Königsberg, Kolmar, Stallupönen

My grandfather, Erich Sehmsdorf, born in Königsberg, apparently was a temperamental and obstinate adolescent. Letters he wrote to his exasperated parents while attending secondary school in the small town of Wernigerode (where they had sent the boy to board with a private family), show rueful awareness that his laziness called his graduation into question (E. Sehmsdorf, 1894-1896). But with renewed effort he filled gaps in mathematics, Latin and Hebrew, and went on to study philology at the University of Tübingen (southern Germany), where he earned a doctorate with a dissertation on Germanic settlements in the Balkans (*Die*

Germanen in den Balkanländern bis zum Auftreten der Goten). The study is still found in international research libraries and wherever German migration studies are taught (E. Sehmsdorf, 1899).

Erich & Käthe Sehmsdorf, 1899

According to my father, Erich became a gifted public school teacher, who knew how to inspire the love of learning. His pedagogical style is evidenced in an article published in a leading education journal, about teaching Paul Heyse's historical drama *Kolberg* (1865) to high school students (E. Sehmsdorf, 1908).

Paul Heyse (1830-1914) was the most prolific and popular German writer after Goethe. In 1910, he received the Nobel Prize for literature "in tribute to the consummate artistry, permeated with idealism" of his enormous output of some sixty plays, and numerous novels, short stories, and volumes of poetry (Nobel, 2023). Among Heyse's historical plays, only *Kolberg* is remembered today, not for its dramatic quality, but for the historical significance of its subject matter, the siege of Kolberg fortress during the Napoleonic Wars (Heyse, 2018).

The five-month siege of Kolberg (today *Kołobrzeg*, Poland) in 1807 cost the lives of thousands combatants on both sides and great suffering among the people of the town. As one of the few fortresses remaining in Prussian hands by the war's end, a heroic myth of patriotic resistance to the overwhelming force of the French invader accrued to Kolberg. The fortress' military leader, Count August von Gneisenau, became a national hero, celebrated during both World Wars (when I was a child,

Wernigerode, Harz district, Saxony-Anhalt

my godfather gave me an intricate scale model of the battleship *Gneisenau* that featured movable gun turrets).

Grandfather's discussion of Heyse's *Kolberg* shows that he appreciated the patriotic message of the play, but was keenly aware of its fatal dramaturgical flaws: weak characterization, illogical plot development, and an externally imposed resolution (*von außen aufgedrängte Lösung*). Given its popular acclaim, however, dropping the drama from the curriculum was not an option. Within a decade after the article was printed, the play had been published in no less than two hundred-twenty editions and performed widely to enthusiastic audiences (Černy, 1919/1920, 376). But neither could a conscientious teacher entertain the play as the great national drama it had become in popular opinion. Instead, my grandfather urged teachers to separate the esthetic critique of the drama from the study of the historical realities behind it. He realized that for most teenagers, it would be difficult to distinguish the literary shortcomings of the play from the significance of its historical content: "The student, the learner, the intellectually dependent (*der Unselbständige*), cannot bring himself to do it if he feels that what the title promises is not kept." If the play is poor literature, how can its message have any claim to truth? However, by reading the play as a historical narrative rather than as a (failed) drama, Grandfather argued, the student can be encouraged to think critically about the Napoleonic Wars and their consequences for Germany.

An avid gymnast, my grandfather also wrote about the physical education programs developed by Friedrich L. Jahn (1778-1852), a German patriot who fought in the Napoleonic wars and became active in the movement for a unified Germany. Known as "Gymnast-Father" (*Turnvater)*, Jahn established a nation-wide network of gymnastic clubs (*Turnvereine*) to build physical strength and patriotism among people of all classes, and he was instrumental in organizing national student fraternities (*Burschenschaften*). Inspired by Jahn, Grandfather promoted the importance of physical education in public schools (E. Sehmsdorf, 1907-1908).

In 1907, my grandfather was appointed "Director of Studies" (*Studiendirektor*) and principal of the higher city school in Kolmar (Polish *Chodzież*), the regional administrative center of Posen Province. Ten years later, he became principal of the Royal High School (*Königliches Pro-Gymnasium*) in Stallupönen (Russian *Nesterov, Kaliningrad Oblast*), in Eastern Prussia.

Königliches Pro-Gymnasium (Royal High School) & the Director's residence, Stallupönen, East Prussia

It is worth noting that my grandfather's appointment was by royal edict. Consequently, when the Emperor abdicated as the result of WWI, my grandfather impulsively resigned his post in protest against what he saw as royal betrayal — only to be countermanded by his practical wife's reminding him that by then they had nine mouths to feed, and economic conditions in post-war Germany were harsh. Incensed, Grandfather removed the portrait of the Emperor from the wall of his study and replaced it with the picture of poet Johann Wolfgang von Goethe.

Erich's stormy courtship of eighteen-year old Erna Mattern (1885-1971) — already engaged to someone else — over one sailing season, ended with their marriage at the end of 1903, with the bride two months pregnant. In June of next year the first son, Georg (1904-1994), was born, followed by my father, Kurt-Eberhard Sehmsdorf (1905-1999), Wolfgang (1906-1992), Lotte (1908-2003), Otto (1910-1979), Fritz (1911-1963), and Joachim (1913-1989).

This reckoning, of course, means that my grandmother by age twenty-eight (her husband thirty-eight) in ten years of active sexual life had produced seven children. Could they go on? My father told us that when Joachim was born, Grandfather suggested that they name the child: "Cross-Reverse-Thyself!" (*Kreuz-wende-dich!*) Grandmother took notice, but how did she prevent future pregnancies in an age before birth control and elective abortion? Apparently by life-long abstention, which illustrates the inescapable conflict between marriage and passion, "the first associated with social and religious responsibility and the second with anarchic, unappeasable love as celebrated by the troubadours of medieval Provence" (Feenberg, 1962). In other words, until the rise of Romantic literature in the eighteenth to nineteenth centuries (and its later Hollywood imitations), marital love remained tied to reproduction and inheritance rather than to personal fulfillment.

By modern standards, life in the Sehmsdorf household was austere, with no indoor plumbing, for example. Water had to be carried into the house from an outside well every day, and the toilet was an outhouse in the backyard. Of course, there was no refrigeration, telephone, or radio. But there was a housemaid who did the cleaning and the laundry, a cook who baked bread and prepared meals, and a

From left: Kurt-Eberhard, Lotte, Fritz, Georg, Otto, Wolfgang, Joachim (1919)

nanny for the children. In typically class-conscious fashion, the maids were addressed with the same informal *"du"* as were the children, while the nanny (*Kinderfräulein*) was addressed with the formal *"Sie"* reserved for adults.

When I was a child, my grandmother once told us how one day when she got up early and went into the kitchen, the cook had already baked bread. The shining loaves were lying on the counter. But the cook wrung her hands. *"Frau Doktor*, I have to tell you, when I came down this morning to finish kneading the bread, the cat had had her litter in the warm dough." "But, Erna," my grandmother, looking at the breads, said, "What did you do?" "Well, of course, *Frau Doktor*, I scraped off the mess the cat had made — otherwise the men wouldn't eat it!" My grandmother refused to tell us whether the family ate that bread. "Bread is sacred," she said.

But in spite of material constraints, the family felt socially privileged in the local community. As my father put it late in his life: "Everybody knew us…We were somebody" (K.-E. Sehmsdorf, 1996). By virtue of his education (*Bildungsbürger*), and position at the school, Grandfather was reckoned a leading citizen in the city. His rhetorical skill as a public speaker meant that his voice was heard in civic and political matters. There was a sense that the family's background as landed gentry gave them quasi-noble status.

A striking example of privilege felt keenly by the children was that they alone were allowed to play freely in the forest adjacent to their house. This forest belonged to Count Königsmarck, who had been friends with Julius Sehmsdorf during the time both of them served as elected representatives in the Prussian Parliament. And so the Count gave the Sehmsdorf family permission to play in the woods jealously guarded by his forester.

Another reason for the family's enhanced social status rested on its military service in the Army and the Reserves. Two uncles of my grandfather had risen to the rank of generals, and one of them had been awarded the rarest military decoration, the *Pour le Mérite*, established in 1740 by Friedrich the Great as the highest order of merit in the Kingdom of Prussia. This honor, awarded no more than two hundred times during WWI, put its recipients (most of them nobles) in the company of major public figures such as Prince Bismarck, Baron von Richthofen, the top-scoring fighter pilot of World War I, or Field Marshal Erwin Rommel, commander of the German *Afrika-Korps* in WWII.

Often this sense of privilege was tinged with social and ethnic prejudice, mostly against Poles and Jews. Servants were thought of as inherently inferior. Why else would they belong to the servant class? They were also excluded from the code of sexual self-control exemplified by my grandparents. One of my father's numberless sayings illustrating social paradigms was: "Every young man has a natural inclination toward the kitchen personnel" (*Jeder Jüngling hat nun mal 'n Hang zum Küchenpersonal*), meaning that kitchen maids were sexual fair game, while mothers and sisters were to be kept protected and pure. The hypocritical sexual norms of the time partially explains why by the eve of WWI, five percent of the German population were prostitutes (Evans, 1976). One unfortunate consequence of this double standard was that my father and his brothers so protected their sister Lotte that she never had a chance to meet any eligible young men, and she stayed unmarried all of life.

As in the rest of Prussia, the majority of the population of Stallupönen were Poles. At the weekly green market Polish was spoken, but in the stores it was German, because the German minority owned most commercial establishments. Polish domestics were assumed to be intellectually inferior, as in the following anecdote recorded by my father: "We had a reception room (*Salon)* in our house, where we greeted our guests. One day our Polish maid invited a street beggar into the *Salon!* My mother of course told her that in the future, she should receive beggars at the kitchen door. What did she do? Next time Count

Königsmark came to visit, she told him to wait outside the back of the house!" (K.-E. Sehmsdorf, 1996).

Poles were also held in suspicion of disloyalty to the Crown. Not surprisingly, really, considering that Eastern Prussia was located on territory seized from Poland by Friedrich the Great. My grandmother once took a Polish priest to task for teaching his young confirmands the song "Poland isn't lost yet" (*Noch ist Polen nicht verloren!*)

Whenever Jews are mentioned in my father's memoirs about his childhood, their description implies dishonesty in business dealings or, if they were welcomed as physicians or teachers, it was noted that they weren't typical Jews. Jewish culinary customs were met with derision, as in the family's habitual praise of a good meal: "It was good and generous, and not as greasy as in other Jewish homes" (*Es war gut und reichlich und nicht so fett wie bei anderen jüdischen Leuten*).

Grandfather was known for his self-deprecating humor. Many anecdotes illuminate his comical perception of his own role in a paternalistic culture. Asked by the children who was in charge at home, Grandfather would thrust out his belly, hook his fingers in his vest pockets and say: "Well, me of course, I make all the decisions in the family." Then he would pause and spread his legs a little further. "Well, actually, I make all the big decisions and leave the little decisions to your mother." And then he would shift his body and let his arms hang down at his sides. "Well, come to think of it, whenever there's a big decision to be made, Mother always turns it into a lot of little decisions." And then he would laugh.

Grandfather was also a strict disciplinarian, and like his forefathers (and the kings of Prussia) would allow himself to fly into towering rages. My father, whose temperament was most like that of his own father, would often bear the brunt of his anger and beatings. My father didn't think there was anything wrong with the beatings and believed that he deserved them,

52

but he noted in his interviews (1996) that he would hide from his father until the latter's ire had evaporated (*sein Zorn war verraucht*), because then the punishment would be more bearable.

street fights they fought together, standing back to back.

At times Grandfather's disciplinarian intentions

Georg, Grandmother, Kurt-Eberhard (early 1920s)

Probably because they were so much alike in their intransigence, neither willing or able to listen or compromise, my father's relationship to his own father always remained tenuous, and he obeyed him grudgingly. He was much closer to his mother, whose loving practicality he valued all his life.

Grandfather pushed his children, for example, by entering them in school at age five, a year ahead of other children. Not every child in the family responded well to this pressure. My father and his sensitive older brother — a musically gifted boy who later became a theologian and African missionary — ended up in the same grade and became inseparable, almost like twins. My father vividly remembered his intense conversations with his brother about God and Christ, but also how in

had comical consequences. When his oldest three sons came to be of a certain age and started climbing out of their bedroom window looking for beer and girls, he countered by locking their pants in his own closet at bedtime. The boys solved this logistical problem by pooling their meager financial resources to buy an extra pair of pants which they rotated among themselves as needed.

Grandfather was a loyal subject of the Crown and he passed his love for the royal house on to his children. My father recalled how as a child he met the Emperor and Empress and was allowed to hand flowers to her Imperial Highness. The colorful troops in their dress regalia, the horses prancing in rhythm with the martial music, the sharp discipline of the marching soldiers, the

Upper row, from left: Fritz, Otto, Lotte, Joachim.
Lower row, from left: Kurt-Eberhard (with facial scar from sword duel), Georg, Wolfgang (1925)

Emperor himself seated on his horse clad in a medieval knight's armor plate, left an indelible impression on the boy. He was equally impressed by the naval maneuvers he witnessed at Binz, the Baltic Sea port on the island of Rügen, and told his father that he wanted to join the navy.

The onset of WWI, however, turned romance into harsh economic reality for the family. Because of his weak heart, my grandfather was rejected by the draft board, and eventually suffered a coronary attack during the war. The substantial inheritance (from his father's share of the manor farm), which my grandfather had used to supplement the typically meager salary of a school principal, evaporated during the hyperinflation in the aftermath of the war. My father, who even as a teenager had more business sense than his own father, had urged him to invest the inheritance in farm land, but Grandfather had laughed at the boy. The Treaty of Versailles foolishly imposed huge debts on Germany that

could be paid only in gold or foreign currency. With its gold reserves depleted, the German government was forced to print money causing the Mark to fall rapidly in value. For example, on the eve of WWI a loaf of bread in Germany cost 0.30 Marks and that price doubled during the war. But under the pressure of paying the reparations imposed by the Allies, one loaf of bread cost 3.50 Marks in 1920, 160 Marks at the end of 1922, and two hundred billion Marks by late 1923. Of course, this wiped out all of the inherited cash Grandfather held in a bank.

Faced with the economic impossibility of sending all three of his older boys to study at university, Grandfather decided to support two of them (Georg to study theology and Wolfgang philology), but he took Kurt-Eberhard out of school at age 15 and placed him in an apprenticeship in a major grain and seed dealership. Even at such young age, my father made use of connections to the family's large grain-producing estates (great-uncle Otto

54

managing nearby Podanin, and great-uncle Hugo the manor farm at Sartowitz), to secure favorable price quotes for his employer, and quickly was given a free hand to negotiate grain deals. Tall, slender, good-looking, an excellent dancer, and from an upper class family, he was welcomed at private dances at the great estates nearby. When the men withdrew to the smoking room to talk politics and business, the boy was right among them, soliciting contracts, and shaking hands. In those days, a handshake was as good as a signed piece of paper.

After my father completed the apprenticeship, Grandfather allowed him to return to school to graduate, on the assumption that he would be able to support himself if he chose to study at the university. In 1925, he began studies in law and economics in Königsberg, while also working for a shipping company. On the side, my father secured a franchise of personal weight scales distributed throughout Königsberg and surrounding cities, and hired a staff to manage the scales and collect the fees. Within three and a half years, he was able to accumulate enough money to finance full-time studies at the University of Göttingen, culminating in a doctoral dissertation on the police authority of the German consul on German ships in foreign ports (*Die Polizeigewalt des deutschen Konsuls auf deutschen Schiffen in ausländischen Seehäfen*, 1932).

During his university studies in Königsberg, my Father became active in a fraternity (*Burschenschaft*) that practiced fencing to develop physical courage and political patriotism. The fraternity required bouts (*pflichtschlagende Mensuren*) with a blank sword and without protective gear other than a leather covering around the mid-body. Facial scars were held in high esteem, especially when sustained during a duel of honor to settle a perceived slight or insult.

In the course of these years — and probably in response to his own father's authoritarianism — my father developed the world view I would equate with Social Darwinism. Like

Jewish philosopher Spinoza (1632-1677), he equated the Divine with Nature (*natura vel deus*). But unlike the Dutch humanist, my father did not recognize the presence of God in nature as Spirit but as the law of survival of the fittest. It was the task of physically and intellectually superior men to shape and guide the lives of the weak, by force, if necessary. No life in nature or in society was possible without hierarchy. As lions rule in noble freedom in the desert, so must strong human beings govern the weak in society.

It is astonishing how my father misconstrued the idealistic poem "The Eleusian Feast (*Das eleusische Fest*, 1798) by Friedrich Schiller. He probably read the poem in school, perhaps under his own father's tutelage. In Father's view, the poem becomes the expression of Darwin's idea that species evolved from the instinctual drive to survive. In his *Interviews* (1996), Father quoted the second to last stanza of this long philosophical poem in which Schiller contrasts the law of nature with that of human ethics. Schiller argued that the "gigantic lusts" (*gewaltge Lüste*) of the animal were contained by "nature's law" (*Naturgebot*). However, for man to be fully human, he must align himself with his fellow man through "his moral law" (*seine Sitte*). There can be little doubt that Schiller meant by moral law what in Enlightenment philosophy and German Idealism was thought to be implanted in human beings by God through reason (most fully expressed in Kant's "Groundwork of the Metaphysics of Morals" (*Grundlegung zur Metaphysik der Sitten*, 1785). For my father, by contrast, moral law was equivalent to social custom and codes of behavior enshrined in law books and the authority of the state. His chosen dissertation topic examining the police authority of the consul was fully consistent with that view. My father had little patience for the Judeo-Christian idea of the moral law enshrining God's command that we love our neighbor, and thereby transcend the instinctual drive of self-preservation. He thought of the New Testament stories and of St. Paul's teachings as social lies invalidated by the execution of Jesus.

My grandfather was an active member of the Lutheran Church, attending services every Sunday, and holding various offices in the congregation. To my father, on the other hand, membership in the church (affirmed at confirmation) was merely a sign of fitting into the customary social hierarchy, without any noticeable effect on his worldview. In this he was like the Teutonic Knights who swore to the love of Christ in the monastic vows they took, but suppressed the populations they were sent to convert. In many ways, Father personified Prussian virtue: he was austere, hard-working, orderly, self-disciplined, tough-minded, courageous, uncomplaining and obedient. However, like the Teutonic Knights he lacked kindness, patience, and compassion. In his old age, he loved visiting our farm on Lopez Island. Often he would take some bread to feed the bluegills in the pond, and invariably would return to announce with satisfaction that "the biggest fish always gets most of the bread" (*der grösste Fisch kriegt immer das meiste*). To him this was the natural order of things, and therefore the moral law.

Interestingly, Father also said: "Thinking begins where prejudice ends" (*das Denken fängt an, wo das Vorurteil aufhört*), but it never occurred to him that his own thinking was riddled with pre-

conceived, unexamined notions. He complained that the generation of his grandchildren, having grown up in post-war Germany, were deeply prejudiced because they were indoctrinated at school, universities, and by the modern media examining Germany's role in the two world wars. In his view, all forms of socialism were false ideas, as the example of the Soviet Union and its satellites showed.

Father defended his dissertation on January 27, 1932, the former Emperor's birthday, as he noted, bitterly, because the newly-baked lawyer couldn't find any legal work in post-imperial and economically depressed Germany. Instead, he found himself carrying pianos up and down stairs for a moving company. After some months, however, he got a temporary administrative job in his hometown Stallupönen, where he mostly had to deal with cases involving support for children born out of wedlock.

During these critical years, Adolf Hitler rose to power in the right-wing German Worker's Party, soon restyled as the National Socialist German Workers' Party, and nicknamed Nazi Party. In 1933, when the party gained the majority of seats in Parliament (*Reichstag*), Hitler was appointed chancellor and quickly passed laws suspending key civil liberties and giving him powers to enact laws without Parliament's approval. A year later, when President Hindenburg died, Hitler named himself head of state (*Führer*), thereby eliminating the last legal means by which to remove him from office.

As part of the economic reorganization of Germany, the Hitler government established the German Agricultural Trade Organization (*Deutscher Landhandelsbund*), later incorporated in The National Food Society (*Reichsnährstand*), to establish legal authority over agricultural production and distribution by a complex system of orders, price controls, and prohibitions based on the claim that agriculture should serve the common good rather than personal interest (*Gemeinnutz vor Eigennutz*).

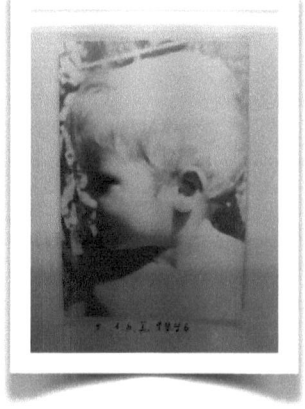

Gernot Schmsdorf, 1942-46

In 1933, the position of managing director of the Agrarian Trade Organization for the region of Königsberg was offered to my father with a salary of three-hundred Marks, to be increased to four-hundred Marks, if he married. He quickly married Ingeborg Seyffarth (1910-2000), the daughter of a senior member of his college fraternity.

It seems that, at least initially, my father misconstrued the political goals of the Agricultural Trade Organization. He believed that it intended to improve production and trade by bringing farmers and distributors together under a shared umbrella. He managed the organization for five years, and was expected to join the Nazi Party, but his application got lost in a bureaucratic tangle.

In 1938, my father was asked by his mother to settle the estate of her own father, Gustav Mattern. Grandmother's inheritance made it possible for her to co-sign a bank loan of twenty thousand Marks. This loan enabled Father to buy a partnership in a paper wholesale company in Heidenau near Dresden (Saxony). It also enabled him to buy shares in a home loan bank (*Bausparkasse*) toward the future purchase of a home for his growing family, including three boys and a girl (Eberhard born 1934, Folker born 1935, Henning born 1937, and Heike born 1938).

In 1939, WWII broke out and Father was drafted into the army. But when a suitable house became available in Heidenau in 1940, he took a five-day furlough to purchase the single-family home and move his family there. The move saved us from certain death by the Allied bombings in February, 1945, which obliterated the apartment in which we had been living in Dresden before the move to Heidenau.

A major portion of my father's *Interviews* (1996) concern his experiences during the war, and how he reestablished himself in business after the German defeat. His war memories circle mostly about his relationship to colonels and generals in the logistical administration of the war, and of the camaraderie between ordinary soldiers. He seems detached from the suffering of the populations on both sides of the onslaught. Almost nothing is said about the relationship to his wife, my mother, whom he divorced when he returned at the end of the war, uninjured in body, but broken in spirit. There is very little reflection about what the family must have gone through, in spite of the fact that three more children were born during the war (Elke 1941, Gernot 1942-1946, and Kirsten 1944), no doubt conceived during military leaves.

Considering my father's consuming interest in all things military during his childhood and adolescence, and his patriotic pursuits while a student, his war career is puzzling. During his last year in high school (1924), he had served three months in the Army Reserves, in response to newspaper reports that restive Poles were stirring public sentiment in favor of restoring Eastern Prussia to Polish control. Prussia secretly rotated sons from "politically reliable families" (*verläßliche Familien*) through summer trainings, and my father was

German Agricultural Trade Organisation

attached to an artillery regiment. He acquitted himself so well that his commander suggested sending him to officer's school, but Grandfather could not afford the cost for special uniforms and other expenses. My father continued training with the Reserves, however, and by the time war broke out, he held the rank of First Sergeant (*Wachtmeister*), and was immediately promoted to First Lieutenant.

Throughout the war, however, my father never fought with a weapon in his hand (*Fronteinsatz*). Rather, he was attached to various regimental commands behind the front lines, wherever the Army needed someone to organize fuel, food and munition supplies, and troop movements. In his role as logistics and ordnance officer (*Bevollmächtigter Transportoffizier)*, he was sent to Silesia, Moravia, Poland, Holland, France, Bulgaria, Romania, Serbia, Greece, and finally to Russia. If he had any ambition to be promoted beyond the rank of junior officer, he probably would have had to request transfer to the front, which he apparently never did. Perhaps, his patriotism notwithstanding, my father understood that to survive the war, it was best to serve by offering his organizational talents from a safe distance (*auf Nummer sicher*), rather than by fighting in the trenches.

In April 1945, with the last German units collapsing under the Allied onslaught, my father fled his regiment, escaping with two sergeants. On the way, the men fabricated false papers identifying them as civilians. Technically a deserter, he buried his uniform in the forest. He did not report to the Allied authorities in order to avoid being taken prisoner. On May 5, he arrived at the house in Bad Harzburg (in the Goslar district of Lower Saxony) owned by his aunt, and there found his own mother, as well as three of his children, including myself, then eight years of age. I vividly remember the bearded man standing by the garden gate looking at me before he disappeared into the house.

Returned to Heidenau to find the rest of his family, my father was denounced to the Russians as a German officer by his former business partner, and had to flee back to the West, then occupied by the Americans, British, and French. He took his family with him, but abandoned the family home, which he managed to sell before leaving.

Kurt-Eberhard Schmsdorf, April 1945

In a first attempt to reestablish himself financially after the end of the war, my father joined an engineer, Dr. Friese, to make wall sheeting from wood shavings and cement. When that business collapsed, he advertised in newspapers and eventually secured a leading position (*Prokurist*) with a firm manufacturing colloid mills. The mills utilized rotating and stationary plates to create a supersonic shear field that blended materials into an inseparable slurry. The machines were widely used in the chemical and food industries.

In order to make himself independent, my father in the 1950s secured the exclusive rights to sell the colloid mills in the U.S., but in the 1960s shifted to chocolate manufacture in Offenbach, near Frankfurt in Hesse. In 1963 he had the brilliant idea to move production to Berlin to benefit from tax savings granted to businesses willing to set up in the city beleaguered by the Soviets. To build a new plant in Berlin, he secured a 450,000 Mark credit under the Marshall Plan, then sold the Offenbach plant to Shell Oil for another 450,000 Marks. With that capital, my father developed the most modern chocolate factory then in Europe and produced two thousand tons of raw chocolate per annum with a staff of twelve, to supply major chocolate makers. By 1972, he sold his shares of the company to Dr. Oetker, the German multinational food company, which in turn sold the production facility to Cargill. My father continued as CEO of the company until 1976. By that time he was already living in the house he built for his retirement in Klagenfurt on Lake Wörthersee in southern Austria, near the border to Slovenia. There he lived until 1988, at which time he joined his brother Wolfgang and sister Lotte in a retirement home in Bad Arolsen in northern Hesse. There Father died peacefully in 1999 at nearly 94 years old.

Life of An Immigrant

Heidenau

I was born in Königsberg, Prussia in 1937. The circumstances of the pregnancy and birth were traumatic, and the consequences for my life dire. According to medical records (*Gesundheitsbogen*), my mother was treated with quinine for venereal disease while she carried me. Concerned about side effects on the unborn child, physicians induced labor repeatedly over ten days, and the birth was difficult. Known side effects of quinine treatments include heart arrhythmia, weakened eyesight, and chronic intestinal disturbances, all of which affected me permanently. The usual childhood diseases: measles, chicken pox, whooping cough, and chronic ear infections were exacerbated by my weak constitution, persistent heart cramps, and massive digestive problems. The constant battle with illness left me "disciplined, pedantic, lacking in self-confidence, nervous, and prone to telling small lies" (*im Wesen diszipliniert, pedantisch, mangelndes Selbstbewusstsein, Nervosität, dadurch Notlügen*). My own memory tells me that I became an introverted child who doubted his mother's love. Craving love and affirmation became signature traits of my personality. Most childhood pictures show me sad and pensive. My inwardness was not well received in my boisterous, outward-turned family. I was considered "a still water" (*ein stilles Wasser*), and my father's assessment that "no one could

From left: Elke, Heike, Henning, Dietmar (cousin), Folker, Eberhard, Christoffer (cousin), Hans-Georg (cousin)

figure me out" *(auf die Schliche kommen)* reflects a moral judgement I struggled with until adulthood.

In 1939, my father took advantage of a business opportunity to move the family to Dresden, and the year after that to nearby Heidenau, where he had bought a beautiful single-family home surrounded by extensive gardens and fields and forests that began at our back fence. The outbreak of WWII removed my father from home life for six long years, except for occasional military leaves, during which my mother invariably got pregnant. My memories of

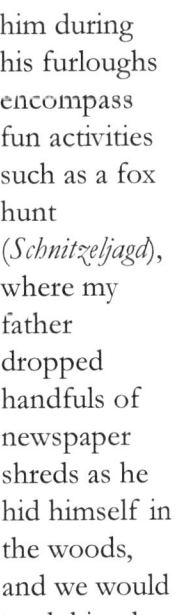

him during his furloughs encompass fun activities such as a fox hunt (*Schnitzeljagd*), where my father dropped handfuls of newspaper shreds as he hid himself in the woods, and we would track him, but

1st Lt. Kurt-Eberhard Schmsdorf, 1939

always failed to catch "the old fox" (*den alten Fuchs*). Invariably he would arrive home before

61

us and have a good laugh at our expense. An excellent gymnast like his own father, he would also show us how to use the high bar and ring-set he had installed in the garden.

Equally memorable, but less fun, were the inevitable investigations when one of his children had committed some punishable infraction, such as breaking off a key in a locked door during rambunctious play, or leaving a footprint on a vegetable bed. Interrogation was made painful by the tacit assumption that children would not tell the truth, and the look of my father's raised eyebrows and his index finger stabbed against my chest, are indelibly imprinted on my memory. Punishment took the form of beating with a thin cane, which we had the good sense of building into a kite and gleefully sending off into the blue sky never to be seen again.

From left: Henning, Folker (in back), Heike, Eberhard, Dietmar (cousin)

Probably because of the size of her family — seven children of her own, in addition to two cousins living with us during the war — and the massive household, my mother had little time for herself or for us, although I vividly remember her teaching us various crafts, working in wood, paper and other materials and helping us set up a puppet theater, for which we built the stage, carved and clothed the puppets, wrote and performed the plays.

Most days, a nanny (*Kindermädchen*) had charge of us as we played in the two large rooms assigned to the children. We were not allowed to enter other rooms reserved for adults, such the master bedroom, my father's study, my mother's studio, the kitchen or even the dining room, which we were permitted to enter only during mealtime. Meals were a formal affair, with children sitting straight on their chairs, learning how to use knife and fork properly. Children were expected to be silent at table "like fish" (*Kinder bei Tisch stumm wie ein Fisch*), while adults carried on conversations about politics, history and other topics, which often required bringing books from my father's library to the table. I loved listening to these talks, and the pleasant habit of conversing with a purpose at mealtime rather than indulging in small-talk, has stayed with me all my life.

Despite the rigorous discipline in the home, access to our garden with a small pool, and the endless fields and woods beyond, filled our childhood with untrammeled adventure. As soon as the weather permitted, we were sent outside, usually without shirts or shoes. We were allowed to go anywhere without supervision at an early age, which gave us a strong sense of self-reliance and independence. We were told that we could climb any tree as long as we didn't fall down and break our bones or tear our pants, and we were permitted to swim in the river at the bottom of the hill (*Kuhberg*) below our house, as long as we took responsibility for each other to make sure no one drowned. I vividly remember my two older brothers and I teaching my sister Heike how to swim by demonstrating the breaststroke on dry land and then tossing her into the water. To this day, Heike recalls that she was not afraid because her brothers were standing by to keep her safe. In the winter, we would hurl ourselves down the same hill on the bobsled we had received as a Christmas gift from

Rough play - From left: Henning, unidentified siblings, Axel (cousin)

our favorite aunt, and we would build igloos in massive snowdrifts behind the house. In the summer we built underground forts with elaborate mazes of connecting rooms covered with planks to hold the soil above us.

The fields and the nearby Kegel Farm were open to us, where we experienced the natural world of animals and agricultural work with an intimacy most modern children cannot even dream of. At times we got into trouble, such as when my brother Folker opened the spigot of a wooden barrel sitting in the field ready to be sprayed on

Opi Seyffarth & Henning, 1939

the soil, and doused us top to toe with stinking liquid manure. Or my brother Eberhard's falling into a manure lagoon and having to be rescued with a wooden pole. I also remember my sister Heike and I, five and six years old, watching animals mate on the farm and experimenting with how mating might work in humans.

Roaming the woods and the fields also seeded my childhood with a deep sense of the irreducible goodness of life, and of the earth from which grows plants, animals, and nourishment, as sacred. The farmer, whose fields we gleaned as children, would gather his household at the edge of the field before planting or harvesting, and say a prayer. His wife would come out midday with a basket of food, unhitch the cow pulling the plough or the spindle flinging the potatoes out of the soil, and milk her to give us the warm, life-giving substance to drink.

My maternal grandfather was a towering presence in my childhood, especially because my father was mostly absent. I loved my grandfather (*Opi*), a retired physician, because he gave me what I craved the most, tender affection and his time. Dressed only in his leather shorts (*Lederhosen*), his white shirt open down to the navel, the white-haired old man would stand in the middle of the shallow pool and sing "Bi-Ba-Butzemann is Dancing" (*Es tanzt der Bi-Ba-Butzemann…*), while we circled

Elementary school in Pirna, now Heinrich-Heine-School, 2018.

around him to play a German version of "Ring Around the Rosy…We All Fall Down." When I was small, he cured my flat feet by carving stilts with slanted rungs for me, and made sure that I walked with the stilts every day until my arches were perfect. And when I fell down, instead of picking me up, he would hold out his arms to come to him on my own. By the time I reached him, the pain was forgotten, and I was happy. If I bled, he would clean the wound with his spittle, blow on it and sing a healing blessing (*Heile, heile Segen…*), which procedure effectively took the place of iodine washing and first-aid bandages.

Our social life during my childhood was completely family centered. There were no phones, radios, television or other social media. My family did not entertain guests for dinner, but there were many visits from close relatives, and some of them lived with us for extended periods of time. The children did not have sleep-overs or birthday parties with their school peers, nor did we ever go out to restaurants, movies, concerts, or theater. We did not go to church, although all the children were baptized in keeping with family custom. We did not take any vacations away from home, or travel as a family.

Christmas and Easter were major holidays celebrated in family tradition, but not as religious events. The children looked forward

to Christmas with almost unbearable anticipation. Partly because of the austerity imposed by the war, but also because of family custom, almost all Christmas presents were made at home. Although she had help from other adults in the house, most of this burden fell on my mother. She wrote and illustrated children's books for us, crafted toys, sewed clothes — often refurbished hand-me-downs from older siblings — knit sweaters and socks, baked cookies and cakes. My mother had the saying, "When Mother lies prostrate on the floor, then it's Christmas Eve!" (*wenn Mutter flach auf dem Fußboden liegt, dann ist's Weihnachtsabend!*)

In Germany, traditionally the Christmas tree was decorated with live candles, apples and wooden toys, a custom I follow to this day. During the war, in addition to the white candles, there was also a red candle in deference to Adolf Hitler, and a blue one to keep our absent father in our hearts. Christmas was set up in the dining room, with the sliding glass doors to my father's study on one side, and to my mother's studio on the other, thrown open to create a very large space. The glass doors to the hallway were taped over with paper, so that we could not see the preparations inside.

On Christmas Eve, the candles were lit and then the children lined up in a row and marched in, the youngest walking first, and the eldest last, while intoning: "Step by step and man for man, our youngest leading the way" (*Schritt für Schritt und Mann für Mann, unser Jüngster geht voran*). Inside, the adults, usually my mother, grandparents, visiting aunts and uncles, the nanny and kitchen maid, would sit on chairs, waiting for us. Each of us would have written poems of our own composing on decorated sheets of paper, and one by one would stand in front of the adults to recite our poem by heart. Then we could turn around and each was led to a place where our presents were covered with white sheets. Presents always included a special paper plate for each child filled with chocolate, cookies and a single orange — the only orange for the year. I remember one year saving that orange for so long that it finally became inedible. On First and Second Christmas Day, fresh candles were burned on the tree while we ate a festive meal of special foods, usually a roast, if the meat could be found.

I remember one Easter, the neighbor's cat made off with the uncooked roast kept cool in an open window (no refrigerator!), and my father, who happened to be home on leave, chasing that cat in his military boots, wildly firing his army pistol, but unable to hit the thief or retrieve the meat. The scene was funny and frightening at the same time, but I don't remember what we ate for Easter that year.

As a child, I went to school under protest. In kindergarten, my reluctance manifested as chronic diarrhea, and I remember receiving a gold star when I finally kept myself clean. In elementary school I recall learning multiplication tables and practicing calligraphy (*Schönschreibung*), both skills neglected in modern education. I also remember being chased by some class bullies and being rescued by scrappy Sonja Ziegler who planted a kiss on my cheek. As there were no school buses, we made the hour-long walk through the village on foot, often shoe- and shirtless, even when going to kindergarten. Of course, there were almost no automobiles on the road then, and traffic consisted of carts drawn by oxen or horses.

Once a week, my mother sent her 4-8 year-old children shopping at a store about half a mile from where we lived. She supplied us with a notebook in which she had written what was needed: bread, vegetables, meat and milk. By the end of the war, food stamps regulated what we could buy, but at times we had to accept

milk or even whey for meat stamps, because there was no meat. Often we had to stand in line for hours to be there in time before all the meat was sold out. The grocer would fill our four-wheeled wooden cart (*Bullerwagen*), and write the cost of each item in the book. Once a month, he would send a bill to the house. Our constant problem was that since we were always hungry, it was difficult to resist digging into the sourdough loaves, and occasionally we would arrive back home with a hollowed-out crust. We grew a lot of vegetables, tree and berry fruits in our extensive gardens, and weeding, watering and harvesting was an important part of childhood. A favorite dessert was fruit from a bush or tree designated by parental permission for the day. Whenever Farmer Kegel harvested grain, potatoes or beets, we were sent to glean behind his workers. We were expected to return our gleanings to the farmer, but then his wife fed us a meal of soup and large slices of bread in exchange. I remember my astonishment when after the

Village entrance to Pirna, 2018

meal, she asked us to lick the wooden soup trenchers, which she then replaced back on the wall shelf.

Memories of my childhood include events people today would consider traumatic. Trauma is an emotional response to events initially producing shock and often long-term reactions, such as unpredictable emotions, flashbacks, strained relationships, and even physical symptoms. Besides the trauma surrounding my mother's health when pregnant with me and the circumstances of my birth and early infancy, I remember at least three experiences in my childhood as traumatic.

One had to do with a woman who stayed in our home for several years. Theo Hoffmann had lost her home during the Allied air raids on Hamburg in 1943. As a public health and pediatric nurse, she was assigned to live with us, presumably on the assumption that she could be of help to a large family during the war. She was a tall, thin, mannish woman with a horsey face and closely cropped hair. I was afraid of her because of her brusque manner and deep voice. She introduced ultra-violet light therapy into our daily routine to activate natural vitamin D production in the skin and help regulate our

Gernot's Grave, 2018

immune systems. I remember all of the children lying naked on a rug wearing protective glasses while under the lamp. She also administered daily doses of cod liver oil containing vitamin A and omega-3 fatty acids, which no doubt helped to improve our health. And she kept detailed medical records of the children (*Gesundheitsbogen*), noting our physical

and emotional development, illnesses and inoculations. She lived in an attic room on the third floor of our home.

One day, I was asked to carry a tray with tea up to her room from the kitchen in the basement of the house. Because of the difficulty of balancing the tray on my hands, I entered the room without knocking, and faced a shocking scene. I saw my mother, undressed, sitting in the lap of Theo, who was stroking her. Stunned, I put down the tray and closed the door behind me. Why the profound confusion and emotional turmoil that I felt? I have thought about this for many years. Obviously, at six years of age, I had no concept of homosexuality, but later came to realize that Theo, unlike my mother, was lesbian. I came to understand that what I saw that day was physical intimacy both women craved, my mother because of her loneliness during the long war, and Theo because her sexual orientation was not condoned in contemporary society, even punishable by law. I eventually came to understand that the shock which left such a deep scar on my emotional life, was due to my profound desire for the intimacy I saw between the two women. I yearned to sit in my mother's lap, tenderly stroked by her. Its lack left a life-long sadness in me that was not relieved until I married Elizabeth.

Another traumatic experience arose from the illness and untimely death of my brother Gernot in 1946. My mother described him as a victim of war. By 1945, all the children were underweight and always hungry. All of us were inoculated against diphtheria, but Gernot developed post-diphtheritic paralysis. I remember my shock seeing the undernourished little boy lose the use of his limbs and eventually even his eyesight and speech as the illness developed into tuberculosis and meningitis. By the time he was hospitalized, it was too late. The physicians rightly pointed out that what the child needed was fresh milk and butter, which were unavailable. He died after a few days.

Gernot was buried in a small white coffin, and the oldest children carried him to the grave. My parents, anticipating that we would have to leave Heidenau, planted a birch tree on the site. In 2018, when Elizabeth and I visited the cemetery where Gernot is buried, we found the grave leveled and unmarked, but the tree had grown beautifully, and it comforted me to think that his life substance survives in that tree.

POW barracks in Neukirchen (undated, anonymous ink drawing)

apartment building where I was living at the time, I found myself waking up, shaking with fear of imminent bombardment.

A year later, we were forced to abandon our home in Heidenau to escape the threat of my father's being imprisoned by the Russians. To make matters worse, my parents divorced, the family fell apart, and the children were spread out all over what then became Western Germany.

A third traumatic experience occurred on February 13-15, 1945, when 1,300 Allied bombers dropped more than 3,900 incendiary devices on the unarmed city of Dresden, killing more than 30,000 civilians in the firestorm intended to terrorize the population locally and nationwide. Of course, we children knew nothing of these facts or intentions. But for two nights we heard the screaming planes and fire sirens over the city, saw the "Christmas tree" flares dropped to illuminate targets, and the hellish conflagration consuming the sky from horizon to horizon. The horrifying vision and sound replayed in my nightmares for decades. As late as in the 1960s in Seattle, when a Boeing plane streamed low over the

Melanchtonschule — Neukirchen & Steinatal

After living briefly in improvised housing, first in Speele, Lower Saxony, then in Hessisch-Lichtenau, Hesse, while my father struggled to reestablish himself economically, the three oldest sons, Eberhard, Folker, and Henning were placed in a boarding school established in 1947 by the Inner Mission of Germany for refugee children. The school was initially housed in a former POW camp in Neukirchen, Hesse, then in 1950 moved to the beautiful Steinatal campus located in a forest surrounded by fields and small villages, near the small town of Ziegenhain.

From 1947-1954, my brothers and I attended the school, which by 1948 under the auspices

67

of the Evangelical Church of Kurhessen-Waldeck took the name of Phillip Melanchthon (1497-1560), a friend of Martin Luther and the first systematic theologian of the Protestant Reformation. I was ten years old when I got there, and during the seven years I stayed at the school, I saw my mother twice. My father found a small apartment in Kassel, about an hour away by train, but had little time to come and see us, and no room for his boys to visit him during vacations. Basically during these long years, my brothers and I were bereft of the parental support necessary for a child's healthy psychological development. Personally, the longing I had felt as a child for an intimate connection with my parents, especially my mother, was left unmet. However, I was fortunate in that at least some of these needs were answered in the social and spiritual climate of the school. Most of the teachers and boarding house mentors were people who lived their faith with kindness and patience. The pedagogical ethos practiced at the Melanchton-Schule could well be described as conforming to the best of the Prussian virtues. Austerity, order, discipline, and hard physical and mental work were matched with unfailing love and empathy.

Favorite teachers, from left: Panten, Hensel, Albrecht, Zimmermann, Klöppel

When the school was still lodged in the POW camp, life was bare-boned. The student body of a hundred boys was organized in four families, with each of two families occupying half of a single barracks. Each half had a dayroom equipped with a wood stove, which we fueled with blowdown from the adjacent forest. The bedroom was unheated, and the straw-filled canvas mattresses in the double bunks were clammy until our bodies warmed them up. Our clothes and shoes mostly came from charities. Food was simple and usually protein-deficient, but the students raised rabbits on grass, pigs on food scraps, and scoured the woods for mushrooms, acorns, wild blueberries, and wild sorrel. CARE packages from America provided supplements in the form of chocolate, peanut butter and occasionally cheese.

The meager diet could not accelerate my physical growth which had been slowed by years of constant hunger in the aftermath of the war. Medical records show that in 1946 my height was about four inches and my weight about twelve pounds below normal. By 1947, I had not grown an inch, and my weight had dropped even more. I suffered from chronic skin infections causing the lymph node in the left groin to swell, and it had to be removed surgically. I remember feeling so good the day after surgery that I made a handstand on the floor, and my hospital gown slipped down over my head, much to the amusement of the boys and girls in the ward. Of course, this ostentatious bravado caused the stitches to tear, leaving a large permanent scar in my groin. Medical examination at the hospital confirmed the congenital heart arrhythmia and intestinal pathology, none of which they could do anything about, except to advise me to abstain from physical exertion. This advice I ignored, determined to make up for any weakness with toughness (*Härte*) and endurance (*Durchhaltevermögen*), two of the Prussian virtues I had absorbed as a child at home.

At the school, I was nicknamed *Pico* (from Spanish, "little bit") after we learned in physics that *pico* was a unit symbol in the metric system denoting a very small factor. Later, reading the historical drama "The Piccolimini" (*Die Piccolomini*) by the classical German dramatist Friedrich Schiller, I was often called Picco Lilliputanus, but never felt abused by that name. The only time I felt bullied was when a teacher called me an "arrogant dwarf." Our music teacher, Herr Münch, was an overly sensitive and volatile soul who took his understandable frustration out on me when a precious brass instrument was damaged by romping boys in a hallway, but I was deeply hurt by his insult, and never forgot it.

Klaus von Heusinger and Henning in Marburg, 1949.

Contrary to the near universal phenomenon of bullying in public schools (and on social media) today, it is remarkable how little there was in our school, if any. If an insult or argument between two boys escalated into a fight, a teacher would gather the class around the adversaries and tell them to duke it out by fisticuffs or wrestling, following rules of fairness that gave even a smaller or weaker opponent a chance to make a stand. After the aggression was dissipated, he would stop the fight and the adversaries would shake hands to end the dispute, after which it could not be brought up again. There was never any disciplinary action involving school authorities, parents, child protective services (which didn't even exist at the time), or the local police.

Non-competitive sports played a central role in our life at the boarding school. The day began with our mentor (*Hausvater*) rousting us out of bed at dawn for a barefoot run and calisthenics in the woods, followed by cold showers. Usually there was no hot water, but once a week a huge kettle was heated over an open fire, and twenty-five boys would take turns scrubbing themselves with a bristle brush in the soapy water.

Everybody played soccer daily, with a wad of rags if we didn't have a ball, and often without shoes. One day, we discovered some abandoned tip-lorries and tracks left behind after the war. With the help of our teachers, and a lot of pick-axe and shovel work, we constructed a soccer field by leveling about 350 x 100 feet of slope below our barracks.

Our sports teachers left indelible impressions on us, far beyond athletic skills. Herr Panten, a tall and austere man, who taught English as well as track and field, often reminded us of the truth of the Latin proverb that "a healthy mind requires a healthy body" (*mens sana in corpore sano*). Our housefather, Herr Hensel, compact and muscular, drilled us daily in calisthenics and long-distancing running. He amazed us with his ability to push himself from a crouch into a handstand, a feat I eventually was able to master. Teaching intern Herr Albrecht, also a good runner, taught us the difference between friends and buddies. He would be our friend, he said, but not our buddy, because the intimacy between buddies easily shaded into disrespect. Tall and thin, Herr Zimmermann taught biology and gymnastics. When I asked him why we practiced risky routines on the horizontal bar, he answered that I would remember the exercise in my old age, when I would still be able to climb trees with confidence. He was right, of course! Herr Klöppel, a former air force pilot who taught math and coached soccer, instilled discipline with quiet patience. Every day, he would write an exhortation on a little strip of paper pinned to his lapel, for instance: "Is that really necessary?" (*Muß das sein?*) When a student's behavior went overboard, he would repeat the slogan of the day, and then he would gather the skin over the boy's arm muscle and give it a little sharp rap that would hurt, but not injure the pupil's dignity.

Friendship loomed large in the emotional landscape of my years at the boarding school, partially replacing the intimacy lost when the family broke up in the aftermath of the war. Some of these friendships, first with other boys, and with the onset of puberty, also with girls, grew into lifelong, deep attachments. In Neukirchen, my closest friend was Klaus von Heusinger, a slow-moving giant who towered above me by at least a foot. Together, we endlessly explored the woods and fields just beyond the campus. One day, we observed some long-eared hares in a potato field and got

Digging a soccer field. Henning with pick-axe, 1948

the idea that if we could catch a couple of them, we could breed them in captivity and eat their offspring. So I chased the hares down the field between the deep furrows, while Klaus waited at the other end, and when the hare appeared before him, he threw himself on top of the animal which clawed at his shirtless chest. We did catch at least one large male and put him in an empty hutch, but the wild animal flung himself from wall to wall. We pitied him and let him go.

What drew Klaus and me to each other was that we both came from broken families. Klaus was the oldest of five children and the only boy in the family, living in a house in Marburg shared with his father, a physician, who was divorced from his mother. Conflict with his authoritarian father was the reason Klaus was sent to the boarding school, and we often spoke about how we missed our families. Because I had no place to go during vacations, Klaus (or rather, his mother) invited me to join them in their already crowded home. One day his mother (*Tante Sigrid*), looking at my face, said that I reminded her of someone and asked me who my mother was. It turned out that they had been best friends during their childhood in Wehlau, East Prussia. Marburg became a second home to me. Klaus' father forced him to study medicine against his will. He became a good pediatrician, but the unresolved conflicts with his father drove him into alcoholism, and he died early.

My brother Folker and I were in the same "family," called the "Rascals" (*Rabauken*), and rascals we were. Since Folker was two years older, but in the same grade, he was bigger and stronger, and the natural leader of our group. My favorite anecdote is about Folker taking us on a late night raid on the town mayor's apple orchard. After lights-out my brother led twenty-five hungry boys in white nightshirts out of the window and to the mayor's garden, where we ate our fill, dropping the rest to the ground. But how to get the apples back to the barracks on the other side of the village? "Pull up your shirts and put the apples in!" Folker whispered. What a sight! Twenty-five butt-naked little boys scurrying through town in the middle of the night! As we climbed back into our bedroom, our housemother opened the door just as the last of us slid back into bed. "What in heaven's name is going on in here?" "Nothing," somebody said breathlessly, and then an apple rolled out from under his blanket and onto the floor. "Well, good night, boys" she giggled, and shut the door.

The neighboring family, the "Dragoons" (*Dragoner*), didn't like their house parents. They didn't think that either of them had a sense of humor and resented the parents' pushing back when the boys were just looking for some fun. Folker offered to "fix them." Up we climbed on the barracks' roof and covered the smoking chimney in the housefather's bedroom with a board, while somebody watched through the window to see what would happen. When smoke poured out of the stove, and the housefather bent over the open stove door, we poured a bucket of water down the chimney. Howls of delight from the roof, screams of

On the left, a scythe for harvesting grain by hand; on the right, an articulated flail for threshing.

outrage from inside, but before the victim could run outside, his tormentors had vanished. We "fixed" the housemother by waiting on the roof with a blanket, and when she came outside to smoke a cigarette in her usual spot, we dropped the blanket over her head. She never tried to find out who was behind this prank.

As a *Gymnasium* (approximately comparable to an American prep school), the school required an entrance examination, which tested language and math skills, and general aptitude. This meant, of course, that children of college-educated parents enjoyed an advantage. My family's discussing history and politics over dinner while the children listened silently, for example, or challenging us to speak High German (instead of dialect), or make calculations in our heads when laying out garden beds or bidding in card games, or

Married women, after church, 1950s

playing chess, gave us confidence to pass the tests with ease. By contrast, I remember, a fellow student whose family's education consisted of learning just enough of the three Rs in a single-room school to prepare for life-long farm labor, felt intimidated among the children of academics. In 1968, the same student looked back on how he had to overcome not only his own sense of intellectual insufficiency at the *Gymnasium,* but also cultural prejudice at home. When villagers said about him, speaking in Schwalm dialect: *"Dä well waß beßres wänn"* (he wants to become something better), they were not paying him a compliment. And when his mother appeared at festive school events dressed in traditional costume, he felt embarrassed.

The interaction between the school and the surrounding tradition communities became an important part of our education. The forests and lovingly cultivated fields of the rolling landscapes of the Schwalm District made a

Woman and children in heritage costumes, 2018

deep and life-long impression on me. In the 1940s-1950s, the majority of the population of the Schwalm — encompassing thirty-five villages and three small towns — were farmers,

Unmarried girls, bibles in hand, 1950s

with a culture of their own, distinct material customs, dress, language, and oral traditions. In the hierarchy of the village, proud farmers married money to money and acreage to acreage, and ruled over the rest of the people. We would see men and women working in the fields by hand, wearing homespun clothes. Married women wore their hair tied up in a knot on top of their heads and covered with a small cap, while marriageable girls let some of theirs flow down their backs. Men wore cotton knee pants and shirts, tight vests, long-shafted boots, and broad, flat hats.

By a generation later, the post-war economy of Germany had profoundly changed regional cultures to transform them mostly into heritage programs, or tourist attractions, but some material traditions survive. In 1989, when my wife and I visited the school, we could smell bread baking from Riebelsdorf, about half an hour's walk from Steinatal. We went there to find the old bakehouse still at the center of the village square, baking bread for some twenty families who prepared the dough at home, and marketed some of the bread to tourists. For some twenty years after the school was established, it relied on the surrounding communities for food supplies, some of them donated by the farmers who sent wagonloads of potatoes, beets, carrots and other crops, which the pupils stored in earth clamps to protect them from rodents and frost. In return, pupils helped with the harvest on the farms. Rural families who were looking to better themselves economically began to send their children to the school to qualify for university level education. The student mentioned above was only the third in his community of eight hundred souls to graduate from the *Gymnasium* after the turn of the twentieth century.

Steina River, 2018

Early on, the school organized no-cost programs in instrumental music, chorale singing and lay theater. I had a good voice and loved singing. To play an instrument, however, families had to be able to afford one, and my parents could not. Both of them were decidedly unmusical, and I had never before been exposed to live or recorded music of any kind, even at home. The group singing of folk and religious songs in the boarding school, trombone and organ music in church, recitals of Bach and other Baroque greats on the spinet by our music teacher, thus were all the more important in opening up a new world to me that shaped my life. Singing, for instance, "Go out, my heart, and seek joy" (*Geh' aus mein Herz und suche Freud*) by Paul Gerhardt during morning prayer, filled me with an unspeakably joyous sense of the presence of God in nature. Or, when at the end of the day, we sang the folk song "Now, brothers, a good night; the Lord in Heaven watches over us" (*Nun, Brüder, eine gute Nacht; der Herr im hohen Himmel wacht*), I felt embraced and safe in a totally new way.

All entertainment at the school was created by the students under the guidance of our teachers. There was no radio, telephone and, of course, no movies or television. Besides instrumental music and group singing, we organized "Colorful Evenings" (*Bunte Abende*), for which we prepared plays, poetry recitals, storytelling, and games. I once played Peter Pan. For Easter and other religious holidays, students rehearsed Passion and other plays and performed them in nearby villages as a thank you for material help received. Getting to a church for a performance often took hours walking, at times in rain or snow. Made hardy by the austere life in the former POW camp, however, we didn't seem to mind. I remember once playing Joseph in a Nativity play at a village church that lay several hours away from the school, and I first had to dry my clothes at the pastor's house.

On Sundays, we usually attended services at Nikolai Church in Neukirchen. The Gothic sandstone structure was built in stages between the twelfth and fifteenth centuries, and since the adoption of the Reformation in Hesse in 1526, Evangelical services have been held there. After church, we liked to go to the fairgrounds and watch the local soccer team battling it out with the team from a neighboring village, bowling in an outdoor alley, or dancing to a brass band.

A seasonal highlight, eclipsing even Christmas or Easter in importance, was the county fair held at Pentecost (*Kirmes*, from Middle High German *kirmesse* = consecration of a church). It was the day or weekend the villagers looked forward to most all year. Apparently the festival originated in pagan times, celebrating the beginning of the agricultural year in early spring. Garlanded farm animals were led through the village, brass bands played, and everyone gathered at a designated inn to eat, drink, and dance. I remember one year a beribboned bull being led to Nikolai Church, where farmers

Boarding House Steinatal, 1950

waited with cows to be bred. Each cow in turn was tied to an iron ring in the church wall exactly at the spot, where inside the church the sacramental wine was kept in a wall tabernacle, and there the bull mounted cow after cow. The ritual made visible to me the unspoken connection held in tradition between the sacred and the sexual act to create new life.

In 1950, when I was thirteen, the Melanchthon-Schule moved to Steinatal, a forested campus in a valley through which flows the small river Steina that became a focus of exploration and

Roommates, from left: Rainer Kempff, Frank Walter, Folker, Hans-Helmut Eisenberg, Hermann von Lösch, Horst Bindseil, Henning

play for me and my friends over the next four years. Until the end of the war, the buildings at Steinatal were a training site for childcare providers and daycare teachers organized by the German state under the Nazis (*Reichsseminar für Kindergärtnerinnen und Hortnerinnen der NS-Volkswohlfahrt*). It may also have been a maternity home for unmarried women under the "Fount of Life" (*Lebensborn*) program intended to raise the birth rate of German children after WWI. Certified "Aryan" (*arische*) women were brought together with "deserving" (*verdiente*) SS-men or soldiers who

had distinguished themselves at the front. An estimated twenty thousand children were born under the program during WWII.

In comparison to the barracks in Neukirchen, accommodations in Steinatal were spectacularly luxurious. Instead of sharing an unheated, drafty bedroom with two dozen other boys, groups of six or seven were now housed in comfortable rooms fronting on a large balcony that ran the entire length of the half-timbered building. Doors and floors were made of solid oak, and hot-water showers the standard. The large, airy dining room on the ground floor became the site not only for meals, but for social events, performances and dances.

The main school building was (and still is) a beautiful brick structure covered with ivy and housing classrooms for an average of twenty-five students. Attached to the back of the school was a large gymnastics hall, outfitted with equipment we could have only dreamed of before.

In hindsight, it is remarkable that during the years I attended Melanthom-Schule, the school staff did not include a school nurse or physician, psychological counselor, or academic advisor. Injuries did occur, of course, but they were met with improvised care. Once my brother Eberhard flew off the horizontal bar while attempting a giant swing (*Riesenrad*), and broke his wrist, thereby blocking the vein that carries the blood back toward the heart. With the artery still pumping the blood to the hand, the latter swelled like a blue balloon. Luckily a physician was on a private visit to the campus, and he was able to straighten the broken bones. Without immediate intervention, my brother would have

Henning & Hans-Helmut, 1950's

lost his hand. My brother Folker was not so lucky. He slipped when climbing a steel ladder and tore off two joints on his pinkie. Without private or public transportation, by the time he reached a hospital on foot, it was too late. He lost the finger. I, too, one day fell off the horizontal bar, but only sprained my wrist. Wrapping a sling around my arm and tying it to the shoulder was all the medical attention required.

Given the risk aversion of modern parents, partly due to our increasingly litigious society's proneness to engage in lawsuits, we shake our heads about such stories. Of course, in the 1950s, there were neither first aid vehicles nor public emergency services in Germany (nor elsewhere in the Western world — 911 was established in the U.S. in 1967). The school could not have afforded to hire medical or counseling staff, or buy the insurance to cover inevitable injuries. But accepting a certain level of risk was also part of the pedagogical concept of the school, in line with the Prussian virtues of courage (*Mut*), toughness (*Härte*), and fortitude without self-pity (*Tapferkeit ohne Wehleidigkeit*), thought to instill a sense of competence and independence in children.

Today "helicopter parenting" is loosely defined as parenting (or school rules) that pay excessive

attention to children's every move and experience. We were largely free of such restraints when growing up. As a result, we enjoyed a larger sense of freedom than that known by my own children growing up in America. We didn't feel the need to push boundaries to the same degree as children in a more controlled world do. Could this be one of the reasons modern adolescents take such outsize risks with sexual behaviors and drug use?

It is interesting that in some societies today risk-taking and resilience are

Henning descending from the high bar , 1950s

deliberately foregrounded in schools and in childhood and adolescent settings as an antidote to the "helicopter syndrome." A recent article in the New York Times described Japanese parents' sending their toddlers down the street to go shopping or visit grandparents on their own. On a visit to Norway, I observed six to eight-year old boys and girls sailing without adult supervision on the Oslo Fjord. My host explained that occasionally there are boating accidents, but they are almost never fatal, and the price to be paid for absolute safety would be too high. Better to risk breaking an arm or falling into the water than to suffer constant guarding and its debilitating effects on personality development.

When the Melanchton-Schule made the move to build a new campus in the Steina Valley, they also ventured to develop a new school program on a co-educational basis. Interestingly, the arguments for and against that decision exclusively concerned the ethical challenges in bringing male and female adolescents together in puberty. No one asked the question frequently raised today, whether boys and girls might actually learn better in segregated settings, because of culturally based differences in learning styles (Schneider, 2013).

The sexual ethos taught at the school was based on the Biblical paradigm, which sees sexuality as sacred and predicated on mutual responsibility. It was recognized that adolescent boys and girls had erotic feelings for each other, but we were asked to keep these feelings to ourselves until ready to take responsibility for a marriage partner. On campus no one was allowed to indulge in overt intimacies, but that didn't keep students from pairing off on long walks into the woods. However, during the seven years I attended the school, I never heard of sexual relations between students. Sex education was minimal. No one worried aloud about confusion regarding gender identity. I remember our biology teacher trying to explain homosexuality by warning against the dangers of infection in anal intercourse, and finding himself confronted with a wall of incomprehension. What was the good man talking about? Flustered, he canceled the lesson. When we sang "Your beauty has made me love you with great longing" (*Das hat deine Schönheit gemacht, die hat much zum lieben gebracht*), we sang in the safety of groups, sharing

Eva 1950s

feelings without the pressure to move beyond longing.

I had three friends in Steinatal, a boy and two girls, whom I loved with the intensity of the young, but each in a different way. Hans-Helmut Eisenberg, the son of a minister, joined the boarding school the same year it set up shop in Steinatal, probably sent there by his parents because of its religious orientation. A year later, Eva Schimmelpfeng was sent to the school for similar reasons, but she attended as an extern, meaning that she continued living at home and came to school by bus every dawn, traveling — as she wryly noted much later — fifteen thousand miles by the time she graduated. Marlies Schwerdtfeger, who attended Melanchthon-Schule for two years, arrived in 1952. She resided in the girls' dormitory established when the school ventured into co-education.

In an essay assignment I wrote in 1953, I described my feelings about Hans-Helmut in startlingly intimate terms. Both of us were taciturn and inward turned, but we opened ourselves to each other in conversation on long walks through the woods to let us reveal the most secret places in our hearts. I responded to this friendship with a joy and empathy I find astonishing in retrospect. I have often thought since that my relationship to Hans-Helmut taught me that love and friendship are fundamentally the same experience, except that the latter is not complicated by sexual feelings. We remained close friends, in spite of my emigration to America, until the time of his death in 2021.

The relationship to Eva was indeed complicated by precisely those feelings to the point of obsession. Eva was a slight and pretty girl, who was as nimble in sports as she was in the classroom, and excelled at playing the French horn. She came from a strict and religious home, and she wrote to me

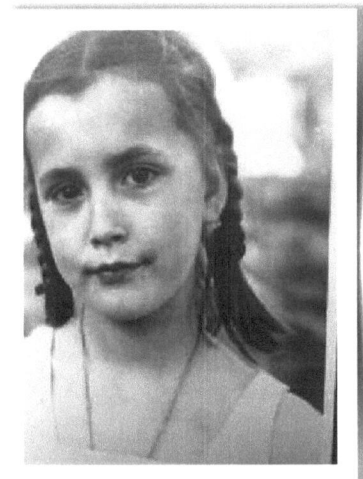

Marlies, 1950's

the year I left school (1954) that she had been afraid of my emotional need, and that the mistake I made was to let her know just how great that need was. Thinking about it later, it came to me that my love for Eva was rooted in trauma, in the sense that it repeated the feeling of unrequited affection I craved as a child from my mother. I was seeking relief from loneliness and from an overweening need for belonging in romantic love and later in marriage. My first experience of love was also my first heartbreak. Unable to accept failure or rejection, I pursued Eva well into my twenties. Obsessive fantasies surrounding her person crowded my dreams for decades and closed me off to finding the love I craved with someone else.

The love and friendship I felt for Marlies was circumscribed this way. Marlies was warm and giving, and her kisses and hugs were a huge comfort to me, but I couldn't love her with the same passion I felt for Eva. Not until much later in life did I learn from Marlies that she harbored unexpressed feelings for me that stayed with her even after she married another schoolmate, with whom she raised a large family. Psychologist Erich Fromm wrote that modern Western culture asserts that love is

outside our control, and our media seem to support this view. By contrast, Fromm viewed the experience of "falling in love" — as I had fallen in love with Eva — as a symptom of narcissistic failure to understand the true nature of love. True love always has the common elements of care, responsibility, respect, commitment, and knowledge (Fromm, 1956). This lesson I was slow in learning, and for a long time doubted the authenticity of any love that came my way.

Academics at the Melanchthon-Schule were broadly humanistic in the classical tradition. The curriculum was organized in three levels (Lower, Middle, and Upper), with students typically being between ten and nineteen years old. Paradoxically the lowest grade was called Sixth Grade (*Sexta*), followed by Fifth (*Quinta*), Fourth (*Quarta*), Third (*Tertia*), Second (*Sekunda*), and First (*Prima*), with the top three grades spread over two years each, for a total of nine years of high school (*Gymnasium*). Academic subjects were cumulative, meaning that at certain intervals, subjects were added and then retained for the remaining years. For example, in foreign languages, everybody started with English at age ten, added Latin at twelve, French at thirteen, and Greek at eighteen. German, mathematics, music and religion were taught all nine years, but political science, history, and geography did not begin until Quarta. The natural sciences began with biology, and chemistry and physics were added later on. Everybody did sports every day. With fewer courses taught at the lower grades, more hours per week were allotted to a given subject in those grades. Later, the larger number of subjects taught each week meant that fewer hours were devoted to each in class, with the expectation that students would devote additional hours of study outside of class.

"Harvest Vacation," 1950s

Instruction was limited to four hours each day, but students would spend as much time again in independent study.

Performance was assessed by assigning verbal grades: exceptional (*sehr gut*), very good (*gut*), satisfactory (*befriedigend*), adequate (*ausreichend)*, inadequate (*mangelhaft)*, and insufficient (*ungenügend*). Handwriting, deportment, attentiveness, and orderliness were also graded. Any student who ended the year with two major subjects graded at the lowest levels, could not be promoted to the next academic level. A student could repeat the same grade twice, but if failing to be promoted a third time, would have to leave the school. Graduation was by written and oral exit examinations proving competence.

Confirmation was an important initiatory milestone on the long walk toward adulthood, and happened usually at age fifteen. For a year, we received religious instruction by a local pastor in the Bible, catechism, and church history to prepare us for taking adult responsibility for our personal and communal religious life. Confirmation also bestowed some material boons befitting our new social status, for example permission to wear long pants, instead of the long wool stockings boys and girls wore as children. Boys got their first formal suit, and were hence allowed to drink beer in public places, for example, at dances. Of course, this meant temptation to flout some established boarding house rules such as bedtime. Confirmed boys would skip out at night to dance the night away at the summer fair, and fall asleep in class the next day. Being confirmed also meant participation in dances held at the school, with the school supplying a bottle of wine for each couple. Students were expected to drink responsibly; if they didn't, they were excluded from school dances for the rest of the year.

It was deeply disappointing to me that my father, for practical reasons, decided that my confirmation ceremony was to take place at a church in Kassel, where he lived, instead of at Nikolai Church in Neukirchen, among my school friends. But my most vivid memory of confirmation is of first communion: taking the blood and body of Christ for the first time so overwhelmed me that I passed out at the altar.

"Harvest Vacations" (*Ernteferien*) on local farms were popular among students at Steinatal. We enjoyed working with our hands and bodies, helping farmers. Harvesting potatoes, and in the evening roasting potatoes over fires burning the dry vines, was a favorite. Students loved sleeping in barns, and dancing at the end of long days of hard labor bringing in hay or grain. It was fascinating to see the hay lifted from the horse-drawn wagons by grapple hooks and disappearing into the open hayloft on a track suspended from the ridgepole. We loved watching solemn men seeding by hand, casting handfuls of grain in great arcs while walking in measured steps across the field.

In 1952, when I was fifteen, my brother Folker and I spent our four-week summer vacation taking a trip on bicycles constructed from junk parts found at the local dump. We painted the bicycles black and outfitted them with panniers improvised from packs we got from the

No-till seeding by hand, 1950's

Shirtless, lederhosen-clad boys taking lunch with two girls met on the road

American Army Surplus Store. A thin, olive-colored Army blanket strung between tree branches served as our tent. We usually bicycled fifty miles a day, but were sometimes able to hold on to the back of passing lorries, which would pull us many miles at speeds up to forty miles an hour before we were discovered by the driver. We made it all the way to the shore of the North Sea and spent unforgettable days on the East Friesian Islands. My father, who was glad that he didn't have to house us during the vacation, supplied us with a lean budget, just enough to feed us, so that we returned several pounds lighter than when we had set out.

In 1953, another great adventure took me and an upper-class student (called Ghandi because he was brown-skinned and thin) hitchhiking in England and Scotland. Our budget was just as

lean, and we mostly lived on a daily ration of fish and chips. In London, a bobby rousted us out of our improvised tent in Hyde Park — no camping allowed in public spaces! In the Lake District, on the English west coast just below the border to Scotland, we spent several days among endless lakes and moors. Having miscalculated our scant food supplies, we snared a hapless hare, but when we roasted our prey over an open fire, found that there was almost no meat on the skinny beast. Faint from hunger, we finally snagged a ride in a luxurious car and the driver took us to his mother's hotel on Princess Street in Edinburgh. Rags to riches! We visited the Tate, the Tower of London, Buckingham Palace, and other museums and historical sites, but nothing compared in memorableness to the challenge of keeping ourselves fed.

Apprenticeship and Emigration — Rastatt and Muncie

My time at Steinatal came to an abrupt end in June, 1954, when my father announced that he could only afford to pay for university studies for my oldest brother, while Folker and I would have to serve apprenticeships and attend trade schools to complete our education. This was bitter for me personally, because, while my high school years had been more focussed on my emotional life than on academic study, I was a better than average student. My father's decision shook me awake and largely motivated me to emigrate to America, where, I had heard, anyone with ambition could achieve whatever he wanted.

For the apprenticeship, my father placed me in the mid-size company of which he was general manager (*Prokurist*). The firm manufactured colloid mills, that is, mills utilizing rotating and stationary plates to create a high shear field that blended the material being ground into an inseparable slurry. The machines were widely used in the chemical and food industries. The apprenticeship involved a formal three-year contract between the firm, a local business school (*Berufsschule*), the State Board of Industries (*Industrie & Handelskammer*), my guardian (my father), and myself. The contract provided for the option of my spending the third year abroad, if qualified.

My training involved rotating between production, marketing, domestic and foreign sales (including English and French correspondence), accounting, bookkeeping, and inventory, and was topped by a stint in the laboratory for quality testing and development. I worked three months in each section, six days a week, under the close supervision of the department head. I was paid the equivalent of $15 per month, and immediately opened a savings account. At the production plant, I

Center: Father, Marianne (mother of Jürgen and Manfred),
Back: Eberhard, Folker, Henning
Front right: Kirsten

mostly assembled colloid mills. To learn about materials and tools, the chief engineer gave me the task of creating an equilinear, six-sided, polished cube (twenty-four ninety-degree angles) from a round steel rod, using only hand tools, a task I worked on for many weeks.

Three days each week, I attended business school, studying German language, expository writing, business correspondence, shorthand, and typing; religion and political science; business administration, math, calculation, and bookkeeping. After two years of study, I was allowed to take the written state board examinations early, and passed. On the day I completed my final oral examinations, I took the liberty to celebrate by drinking beer at a local pub in the company of other newly minted industrial journeymen, only to be remanded by the boss, my father, who insisted that I spend the rest of the day working at the office.

The offices of the firm were located on the ground floor of a four-story building in Rastatt, a small town in Baden-Würtenberg that had been the residence of the Counts of Baden-Baden. Our family lived on the second floor of the house, and the third and fourth floors were occupied by middle management employees. In 1952, my father married Marianne Kempff (1921-1988), a war widow, who had a son named Jürgen (1944-2009). My brother Manfred was born in 1953, which means that the family consisted of five brothers, and my sister Kirsten (1944-).

Our apartment was crowded: besides the small kitchen and a single bath, there was a dining room which doubled as a bedroom for the youngest boy and girl, while the three oldest boys resided in a small bedroom outfitted with double bunks, a desk, and an armoire. When Manfred was born, my father built a tiny nursery in a walk-in closet in their bedroom. My father and stepmother reserved a formal sitting room for their own use, and my father reserved the study where he kept his books, for himself. In the sitting room there was a small record player, and I would sneak in there at night, and lie on the floor to listen to classical music.

Bereft of the intellectual atmosphere of the Melanchthon-Schule, I felt socially and culturally isolated in Rastatt. Being an apprentice meant that I now moved among

Rastatt town ramparts on river Burg, 1950s

blue-collar workers who had different interests than my former peers at the school. Nevertheless, I became close friends with Norbert Winter, also an apprentice, and son of a day laborer. On Sundays, we took endless walks along the ancient town ramparts and on the dikes of the River Murg. One day, we stopped by his house, and I was shocked by the flaking, water stained walls, and primitive furnishings. In turn, Norbert's mouth dropped open when I showed him my parents' sitting room in the apartment, adorned with Persian rugs, polished furniture, and silver serving dishes displayed behind glass. The social gap

between us became painfully plain when I invited him to have dinner with us, and my father forced me to cancel the invitation.

Negotiating my budding sexuality proved difficult during the apprenticeship. The blatant sexism and crude jokes at the workplace bordered on what today would be considered harassment. Erika F., my father's secretary, a twenty-five year old, voluptuous woman married to neglectful man, pursued me into hidden corners at the office, and pressured me for sex. Or was it love? Erika wrote to me that I was her "soulmate" (*Seelenpartner*); but she was married, and my heart belonged to Eva! In a letter to Hans-Helmut in 1955 (H. Sehmsdorf, 1955-2021), I wrestled with my confusion, quoting WWI poet Walter Flex (Flex, 1917): "Staying pure and maturing — the most beautiful, most difficult art of living" (*Rein bleiben, reif werden; schönste, schwerste Lebenskunst*).

Later on, in America, I was reminded of Erika when I saw Mrs. Robinson in *The Graduate* (1967). Of course, the graduate in the film was several years older than me, and his seducer easily persuaded him to put aside his qualms about marriage infidelity. Half a century later, a German journalist ridiculed Walter Flex as an insufferable "apostle of truthfulness" (*Wahrhaftigkeitsapostel*), and castigated his idealism about the Prussian virtues as proto-fascist (Krause, 2013). In the post-modern world, sexuality had been mostly uncoupled from the values Fromm had foregrounded in *The Art of Loving* (H. Sehmsdorf, 2023). But at barely eighteen, my moral compass was firmly set by the sexual ethos I had absorbed at the Melanchthon-Schule. In my conundrum, I had confided in my father. But he had simply laughed at me, implying that I might as well take advantage of my opportunities. Years later, however, I reflected on how my father's own marital infidelity had impacted my life by infecting my mother with venereal disease while she was carrying me.

During the summer of my second apprenticeship year, my friend Norbert and I spent several weeks hitchhiking to the west coast of France. Later in the year, I met John M., originally a German immigrant who had become the twelfth largest meat packer in the U.S. He had come to Rastatt to buy several colloid mills. I told him of my dreams of higher education, and he offered me a job at his plant in Muncie Indiana, assuring me that with hard work, I could fulfill all my dreams in America. Within a few weeks, he secured Green Cards both for me and for my brother Folker, who at the time was apprenticing in a coal mine in northern Germany.

Nineteen-year old immigrant, 1956

Before leaving Germany, I sought out my closest school friends, Hans-Helmut, Marlies, and Eva, to say my farewells. I had been in touch with them by letter after leaving the Melanchton-Schule. Eva would not see me. Visiting Marlies, by contrast, I got an inkling of her deeper feelings for me, but could not respond to her because my (broken) heart belonged to another. Also, with my future in America uncertain, I was not able to make plans beyond the wish to continue our friendship. I went on corresponding with Hans-Helmut for more than fifty years, and we visited each other a number of times.

From our savings, my brother and I bought passage on the Dutch emigrant ship *Maasdam*, which sailed from Rotterdam in September, 1956. The journey across the ocean felt like being suspended in time. We sailed through a heavy storm, but I did not get seasick. Arriving on Staten Island nine days later, we transferred to a train for Chicago, from where we flew to Muncie, Indiana. There we found lodging in the home of Mrs. Elam, right across the street from the packing plant.

Working at the meat plant proved nightmarish for me, while my savvy and practical brother soon found a niche installing and running the colloid mills purchased for adding maximum levels of water to processed meats, such as hotdogs, sliced bologna, and other sausages. I was appalled by the unsanitary and unsafe working conditions, by the stench emanating from the plant that could be smelled in much of the city, and by the effluents running into the water of the nearby White River. I was horrified that cattle were

Emigrant S.S. Maasdam, 1956

bludgeoned to death with sledges, and hundreds of pigs every day were doused with water and crowded together by touching them with electric prods. Rushing forward, they were caught by one leg with an iron hook attached to a continuous chain that ran through a wide tube and lifted the screaming pigs up to the kill floor above, where they were dispatched by a cut to the throat.

I did not have a fixed job, but rotated daily wherever needed, from the refrigeration rooms, where I pushed huge beef carcasses into freezers, to the hot dog stuffing rooms, where women made lewd jokes at me, to the spice room, where my job was to read labels and recipes for the sausage maker who, bizarre as that may seem, was illiterate, although he had graduated from high school. At one end of the plant loomed huge kilns in which the offal was incinerated. One day, I was told to clean out the kilns, shovel the stinking ashes into a semi-truck, and take it to the city dump. I had earned a driver's license on a VW Beetle just before leaving Germany, but had never driven a car of my own. Undeterred, I managed to maneuver the monster, but when dumping the load, fell into the garbage pit and cut my back on broken glass. So I was taken off that job.

Diminutive Mrs. Elam rented a small attic room to us, and put copies of *Playboy* under our pillows. She was the wife of a traveling salesman, a burly red-haired man, who came home every weekend and loaded us all into his Oldsmobile Cabriolet to get an ice cream. We were invited to watch television in their living room, and marveled at Elvis Presley grinding his hips on the Ed Sullivan show, or at Adlai Stevenson running for president against Ike Eisenhower. I liked Eisenhower (originally Eisenhauer, an old German word for smith) because of his Pennsylvania Dutch background and because of his direct and honest communication style I associated with German culture. But I preferred Stevenson because of his intellectuality.

Since we didn't have kitchen privileges in Mrs. Elam's house, my brother and I ate most of our meals in a greasy spoon right at the entrance to the meat plant. But on Sundays we walked to the closest Howard Johnsons, located at an intersection to the interstate highway running through town. I attended a nearby church, and found myself warmly welcomed by the congregation, but to my amazement was not allowed to shake hands with the white-gloved and hatted women. About an hour's walk away from our lodging, Folker and I discovered a skating rink. I met a girl there and asked whether I could take her out on a date. Next Sunday afternoon I walked to her parents' house, dressed in my confirmation suit, and with flowers in hand for her mother. To my shock, however, the father sent me packing, without explaining why. I suspect that he was put off by the foreign formality of my social gesture, and perhaps also by the fact that I didn't come driving a car. What was I going to do with his teenage daughter, if not take her for a spin to the popular drive-in theater, where most young people hung out on dates?

Soon after arriving in Muncie, I discovered Ball State Teachers College (now Ball State University), and enrolled in an evening course in English. Once during a discussion about baseball, I asked what a "rookie" was, but my question was met with howls of

Webster's 1956

laughter. "You're a rookie," someone finally shouted, but that still left me in the dark. The next day, I bought *Webster's New Collegiate Dictionary*, which I carried with me from then on until the book fell apart. Writing papers for the class would have been impossible without that dictionary. English boasts the largest vocabulary of any language in the world. For example, having been assigned to characterize the figure of Kurtz, an ivory trader in Joseph Conrad's *Heart of Darkness* (1899), I struggled whether to describe him as regal (from Latin *regis*), kingly (from Anglo-Saxon *cyng*), or royal (from Norman French *roial*)? The three terms originally meant the same thing, but overlaid in English by successive conquerors of the British Isles, each took on a different shade of meaning. Webster enabled me to distinguish those meanings. I concluded that Kurtz, who "had gone native," was a "regal" representative of Conrad's idea that there is little difference between so-called civilized people and savages. It felt wonderful to be back in school, exploring ideas.

Our social circle widened greatly when Herma Miller, the vivacious German wife of a local veterinarian, heard about the "two German boys" in the neighborhood. The Millers practically adopted us, and in 1958, when Hanne, the beautiful younger sister, came visiting from Germany, Folker immediately fell in love with her, and they married a year later.

Charles Harrington Hightower III, 1957

Early in 1957, my brother and I received letters from Uncle Sam informing us that as foreign residents of the U.S., we were subject to the draft. We could choose between enlisting for six months of infantry training, followed by four and a half years in the Army Reserves, or taking our chances with the draft lottery. I welcomed the opportunity of six months in the military, during which time I could reflect on next steps in getting an education. My brother, on the other hand, who felt more embedded in his job at the meat packing plant, did not enlist, and eventually was drafted for three years of service. He had a gift for soldiering, though, and quickly rose through the ranks to become a sergeant and then a First Lieutenant and Company Commander, even while still a German citizen.

For Basic Training, I was sent to Fort Leonard Wood, a muddy hellhole in Missouri, populated with black-moccasin snakes, snapping turtles, and mean drill sergeants. Once, when we were running uphill in full battle gear in hundred and twenty degree heat, firing our guns at an invisible enemy, our sergeant ordered us to shout "Kill! Kill!" I was running silently, and the sergeant running next to me, threatened to court martial me, if I didn't shout. "Fuck you!" I screamed at him, and he was satisfied with that expression of aggression.

While in the Army, I met a man who became one of my best friends in America. Charles Harrington Hightower was a beautiful tall Black man, a Quaker, who held a master's degree in social studies from the University of Chicago, and he spoke fluent French! I shared a work desk with him at regimental headquarters which he practically ran for the usually drunk sergeant major. The sergeant was embittered over having been field-promoted to colonel during the Korean War, but forced to return to enlisted rank at the end of the war.

During our time off from duty, Charles taught French language and literature to fellow soldiers at the camp, and I became his assistant. He invited me to visit his family in Chicago, where his father was a lawyer, and he took me to see the campus of the University, a life-changing experience for me. Several years later, I enrolled at the University, where I found the educational home I had been looking for, and earned both master's and doctoral degrees there. Our friendship came to an end when Charles revealed to me that he craved a sexual relationship, and when I refused, he felt misled. To me, friendship meant emotional intimacy, but I was not attracted to men sexually, as I was to women. I came to understand that what separated us was a deep cultural difference in the perception of male friendship.

University: Rochester, Frankfurt, Chicago

To make himself independent, my father in 1956 secured the exclusive rights to sell the colloid mills in the U.S. In 1957, he established an office in Rochester, New York, and bought himself a house, where he lived with his wife and youngest son. By the time I finished Basic Training, he put me in charge of marketing, correspondence and accounting for his business, and my brother of machine installation and service. When I arrived in Rochester, I found to my surprise that Marlies was there to work as an office assistant, presumably at her initiative.

I applied to the University of Rochester, and by 1960 earned a bachelor of science degree, attending both day and night classes, as my job allowed. Rather than focussing on professional goals through a specific major, my studies concentrated on how reality is construed in philosophy, science, art and literature. I was lucky that the University of Rochester was the academic home of Lewis White Beck, then the greatest living expert in America on the philosophy of Immanuel Kant. He introduced me to Kant's critique of Descartes' separation of matter and mind, and of the consequent epistemological skepticism of the English pragmatists. I was also lucky in becoming close friends with a fellow student of philosophy, Winston D., who later took graduate degrees at Harvard and the University of Chicago, and taught philosophy of religion in the U.S. and Japan. He dedicated his last academic book, on comparative ethics, to me, calling me "the first philosopher I ever knew" (Davis, 2001). Together, we poured over Kant's complex writings, reading them side by side in German and English, our brains smoking.

Eventually, my father realized that neither my brother nor I were going to make permanent commitments to his business, and he pulled up stakes in the U.S., giving the house in Rochester to my brother, who by then had a young family. With our relationship still open-ended, Marlies returned to Germany. I found lodging in basement apartments, trading yard work for rent, and worked summer jobs as a house painter during the day and selling hotdogs at night to earn enough money to attend college during the academic year. After a year, the University of Rochester generously awarded me a tuition scholarship. Then, during my last year as an undergraduate and the first as a graduate student, I found employment with the Episcopal Diocese of New York. I worked as the driver for the bishop during the academic year, and during the summer as his secretary and gardener at his palatial residence in Maine. This part-time position afforded me plenty of time to study, but little for the usual social life of a student. I had limited financial means for dating, quite aside from the fact that the continued obsession with Eva overshadowed any potential relationship to the women I met.

Not surprisingly, I felt disconnected from the youth revolution in the United States, notably the social and cultural movement during the 1960-1970s that resulted in liberalized attitudes toward sex and drug use. A fellow student offered me LSD, promising that if I took the drug and then held my head under a running water faucet, it would feel like I was standing under Niagara Falls. To me, it seemed absurd to take a drug to simulate an experience I could have — and did — by driving the short distance from Rochester to Niagara Falls. Nor did I feel the need to rebel. Having emigrated at age nineteen, I understood the link between freedom and responsibility. I was fascinated by E. F. Schumacher (1973, 1977), Frithjof Capra (1975, 1982), Herbert Marcuse (1964), all of them German- or Austrian-born and -educated, but writing from within North American culture, and calling for social change and cultural freedom based on holistic ecological perspectives and human-scale economics and technologies. But I thought that the youth protesters childishly confused freedom with the license to engage in "liberating" activities in defiance of parental or state authorities.

I later often reflected on how the Prussian virtues I had absorbed as a child and adolescent helped me through these years of economic hardship and social isolation without feeling burdened or disadvantaged. However, in 1961, five years after emigrating to the U.S., I found myself so overwhelmed by loneliness and homesickness that I returned to Germany to assess where I should settle permanently. I longed to hear the sound of my native language. I wanted to speak frankly without offending. I wanted to have my sardonic humor understood. I didn't want to feel like a stranger all the time.

In exchange for help rehabilitating an old house he had purchased, my father offered me room and board in Hanau, Hesse, about fifteen miles by train from Frankfurt. The proximity of the University of Frankfurt, and the fact that no tuition was required, allowed me to continue studies in philosophy and literature there. I thrilled to Adorno's year-long lectures providing a synthesis of Romantic science, philosophy, art and poetry, which led me to write a master's thesis on the work of Novalis (H. Sehmsdorf, 1964).

Theodor Adorno, a Jew who had returned to Germany after WWII, was a fascinating thinker and musicologist. He was a leading member of the Frankfurt School of Critical Theory that based its critique of modern society and culture industry on the works of Hegel, Marx and Freud. However, unlike critics who rejected much of German tradition as proto-fascist, Adorno labored, albeit controversially, to rehabilitate the Romantic poets, especially those whose lyrics had been immortalized in "Lieders" by Schubert, Schumann, Brahms, Wolf, Strauß, and Offenbach (Adorno, 1961, 105-143).

My father, however, remained skeptical of humanistic study, and offered to support me only if I took a degree in law. Instead, I applied for a scholarship from the University of Chicago, and returned to the U.S. to spend six intellectually delirious years to earn a doctorate in the Program in Comparative Literature. The University was the home of the Chicago School of Critics. Novelist Saul Bellow taught about postmodern fiction, and Protestant theologian Paul Tillich expounded on all religions as attempts to comprehend "the ultimate ground of being" (Tillich, 2015). Mircea Eliade and his colleagues in anthropology lectured on mythological patterns in cultures and literatures (Eliade, 2019). The great classicist Richard McKeon introduced me to Aristotle (McKeon, 1941). The world of art and sculpture offered by the Art Institute downtown, and by the Oriental Institute on campus, the world of music available to me through the Chicago Symphony and the jazz alleys downtown, where Muddy Waters and other jazz greats played, provided sensory complements to what I learned from books about how spirit and matter relate in human experience.

While studying how world view was construed in pre-industrial culture, I came across a correspondence between German philologist Jakob Grimm and Norwegian folktale collectors. Grimm wrote enthusiastically that nineteenth-century Norway had preserved old understandings of self and nature no longer available in industrialized Europe, and that these could as yet be found among fishermen, farmers, and foresters still making their living in close proximity with the natural environment. I decided to learn Norwegian (and other Scandinavian languages and dialects), so that I could study those oral and material traditions in the original.

For several years I took courses in Scandinavian languages at the University of Chicago as well as summer courses at the University of Oslo. In 1966, I received a Fulbright scholarship to spend a full year in Oslo, studying folkloristics and how mythology and tradition inform literature, with emphasis on the cultural revival of Norway after its independence from Denmark in 1814. I ended up writing my doctoral dissertation on the peasant novels of Bjørnstjerne Bjørnson (1832-1905), and how he used folk speech, folk narratives and belief traditions to create a new national idiom (H. Sehmsdorf, 1968).

U.S. citizen, 1963

In one of the Norwegian language courses at the University, I met Jean K., a doctoral student in anatomy, who became one of my closest friends. Jean's family background was as fraught as my own, and we understood each other intimately. During the year in Frankfurt, I had tried and failed to renew contact with Eva, and I knew that I must move on. So in 1967, after I passed my Ph.D. examinations and was offered a tenure track position at the University of Washington on the West Coast, but Jean had to stay in Chicago to complete her own work, we decided to get married, trusting that our friendship would eventually blossom into marital love. We did not see each other for nearly a year, however, and by spring of 1968, Jean called me to say that she had fallen in love with her dissertation supervisor. As a practicing Catholic, she needed permission from the Church for a dissolution, which did not prove difficult, because the marriage had not been consummated. The civil divorce simply took a mutual declaration before the court.

The six years in Chicago brought me face-to-face for the first time with socio-economic inequities, racial tensions, and political violence in America. Students were warned to stay out of the slum districts just south of Midway (since then the University has bought and incorporated the entire area). Our living in privilege next to a neighborhood in extreme poverty and distress created not only tension

but outright fear. Occasionally this fear found relief in encounters that would be comical if they didn't express deep underlying distrust and anxiety. For example, during the first year of my stay at the University (1962), I lived at International House, where I rubbed shoulders with students from around the world, among them two students from the Soviet Union. These two young men quite deliberately ventured into the slums to see for themselves the underbelly of capitalist America. They were promptly held up at knife point, but when they held out the only money they had, which were rubles, the would-be robber refused them saying that "he didn't want to give these Commies the wrong impression of America." What a howler the Russians told fellow students over coffee!

After my stay at International House, I moved together with fellow student Benjamin R. (a lanky fellow from New England who later became professor of religious anthropology and provost at the University of Virginia), to the slums south of Midway, probably from some naive refusal to accept the blatant racism infesting Chicago, as it did most American cities. So one day, I was walking across the skybridge encased in hurricane fencing to keep people from throwing things on the cars below, which spanned the multi-lane super-highway separating the university campus from Jackson Park on the shores of Lake Michigan. When I got to the top of the stairs and entered the "tiger cage," I saw a large Black man enter from the opposite side. This made me nervous, but I kept on going, clutching the pocket knife in my jacket. We met in the middle of the claustrophobically narrow space of the cage, and bumped into each other. I felt for my watch — it was gone! In a blind fury I turned around and shouted: "Give me that watch!"

And the man did! I stuffed the watch into my pocket, stomped around on the beach at Lake Michigan for a while, returned back to the apartment still in a white fury, where I told Benjamin what had happened. "But, Henning," he said, "there's your watch lying on top of the dresser!" So this is the only time I've been held up in all the years since I immigrated sixty-eight years ago!

My sojourn at the University, of course, also bracketed that tragic Friday on November 22, 1963 when President Kennedy was assassinated, just about a year after I arrived in the city, and nine days after I pledged allegiance to America by becoming a citizen. Like most Americans alive at that time, I remember exactly where I was at 12:30 pm, walking out of the L-station near the

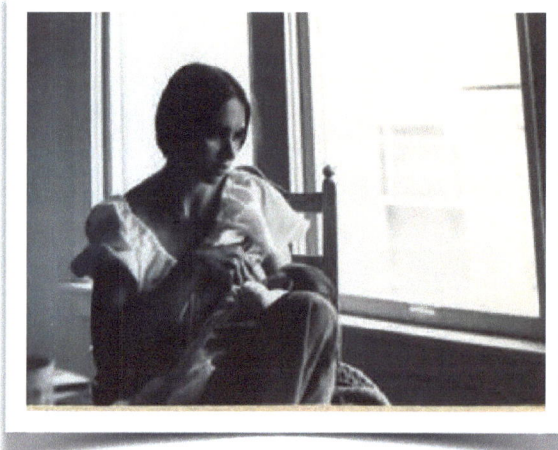

Sally nursing Käthe, 1974

Chicago Museum of Modern Art. The racket of the trains rattling overhead was suddenly pierced by a hysterical scream coming from a man running out of a nearby store with a portable radio in his hand and shouting "the President has been shot!" People massed around the man, moaning, wailing, cursing and standing in silence until half an hour later, the strangely calm voice of a reporter from Dallas announced that Kennedy had died. Elizabeth, then twelve years old, remembers the announcement in her classroom at school in her home town of Hood River, Oregon. "It was as if all the air had been sucked out of the room…I couldn't breathe!" I don't recall how or when I got back to campus that afternoon or what happened then. I felt dazed by the incomprehensible enormity of the murder of

this young president who had so memorably challenged his countrymen to put country before self interest.

Seattle: University of Washington

In Seattle, in the fall of 1968, I met Sally K., the future mother of my children. At age thirty-two, this was my first real sexual relationship, apart from fumbling encounters in the past, all of them abortive because the essential element of mutual commitment was missing. We were married in 1969, and five years later our first child, Käthe, was born, and two years after that, Johann. In spite of our love, however, the marriage was not successful because we did not have the maturity to listen to each other with empathetic, open hearts. We struggled with our demons, but after thirteen years felt compelled to separate. We divorced five years later, after Sally had completed her professional training. During that time, our children lived in the family home while we took turns caring for them. I am deeply aware that the divorce has been as damaging to them, as my parents' divorce had been to me.

Having failed repeatedly to find a permanent life partner, I slowly came to realize an underlying inability to recognize love when it was offered. To a degree I had not known before, I opened myself up to new relationships, always searching for the committed intimacy I yearned for. I failed again and again, because of insurmountable differences in age, culture, geographic distance or other impediments. My search finally ended when I met Elizabeth S., with whom I collaborated as a colleague at the University for two years before we discovered that she was a widow, and I a single father. The key to the success of our marriage over the last thirty-five years has been that we have learned to love and accept each other as we

Fatherhood, 1974

are, without judgement. Together, we learned that to love is to give yourself, and to take care of each other.

I loved teaching at the University, and I loved the research. Between 1967–1994, I held appointments at UW in the departments of Scandinavian Studies and Comparative Literature, teaching Norwegian language and Scandinavian literature, folklore, mythology, and their interrelation with literature and culture, and published studies on those topics in various journals and essay collections in the U.S., Scandinavia and Germany. In 1974, I earned tenure with a short monograph on the use of myth in Knut Hamsun's modernist novel *Pan* (1894), published in a separate issue of *Edda*. I also published volumes of translations of Norwegian fiction (1986) and drama (1989), and for three years, became department chair. Between 1988-1999, I published three volumes of critical texts on Scandinavian folk tradition, folktale repertoires, and the theory of Nordic folklore studies.

In the 1980s, I joined the Washington Folk Life Council and eventually became its president. The Council held annual conferences on traditions in the state, and in 1989 published *Folk Arts of Washington: A Survey of Contemporary*

Folk Arts and Artists in the State of Washington (edited by state folklorist Jens Lund, in collaboration with Elizabeth Simpson). In 1991, I brought the journal *Northwest Folklore* from the University of Idaho to UW (supported by a grant from Skaggs Foundation). In 1986, I offered an ad hoc Ph.D. program in folkloristics through the Folklore Research Division of the UW Center for the Humanities, and started field work courses to collect Scandinavian traditions in the Pacific Northwest, with the data published in *Northwest Folklore* and in journals in Scandinavia and Germany. In 1989, I published the personal narratives of Norwegian-born fisherman Fred Simonsen in the German folk narrative journal *Fabula*, and lectured on the topic in Göttingen, Bergen, Helsinki, Prague, Budapest, Vienna, and Munich. After retirement from the University in 1994, I published an update on field work studies of Norwegian traditions in the Pacific Northwest (2020), followed the same year by a volume of essays summarizing work on how traditions continue to shape cultural life.

Lopez Island: S&S Homestead Farm

Parallel to my work at the University, I looked for a place where I could raise and feed a future family. A major reason I accepted the position offered by UW were the endless forests and plentiful open farm land surrounding Seattle. I envisioned teaching in the city, but living on a farm in the country, where we could grow our own food, and kids could run free. It was a vision of life free of the transactional market and ruthless competition, a life of physical and ecological health, where spiritual and material needs could both be met. This dream began when I saw how food was degraded at the meat plant in Muncie during the 1950s, at a time when America turned to a corporate food system compromising nutritional quality for the sake of convenience, choice, and the lowest possible price. What I observed working at the meat packer contradicted everything I had learned during my childhood and adolescence about the sacredness of food and the earth from which it came. I resolved that if I were to eat meat in the future, I would have to grow it myself. In the 1960-1970s, that dream was supported by the Back-to-the-Land-Movement's calling for small-scale food production for greater self-sufficiency and community autonomy, a movement that had roots in what in the 1920-1930s was called Distributism, and was an attempt to find a third way between capitalism and socialism.

In the mean time, however, federal agricultural policy had pushed the food system in the opposite direction. Earl Butz, Secretary of Agriculture under Eisenhower, Nixon and Ford, abolished the program that paid corn farmers not to plant all their land in order to prevent low corn prices. His mantra was for farmers to "get big or get out" (Scholar, 1973; Carlson, 2008) and grow commodity crops "fencerow to fencerow," instead of feeding themselves and their communities. The rise of major agribusiness corporations precipitated the financial decline of the small family farm and directly caused the American diet to shift to corn-derived products such as corn flour, cornmeal,

Logging 1970's — from left: My father, Henning, Dieter Rautenhaus (husband of sister Heike), Gernot (Folker's son), Folker

cornflakes, corn oils and syrups, dextrose and fructose, and animal feed for dairy, egg, chicken, beef, pork, and lamb production. The massive shift from omega-3 proteins in grass-based foods and feeds to omega-6 proteins in corn had huge, long term effects on public health, causing obesity, lowered life expectancy, diabetes, cancers, ADHD, and related diseases.

Beyond ecological and health considerations, there was another motivation for my search for a rural lifestyle. As an immigrant, I was quite literally looking for a way to put down roots in this foreign land. Ever since reading about the cultural history of America, I was impressed by Thomas Jefferson's argument that the independent yeoman farmer was the backbone of democracy because he could freely speak his mind and vote his conscience (Onuf, 2001). Standing at the edge of the property when I had sealed the purchase, I was both elated and frightened by the prospect that this was the place where I would make a lifetime commitment. I would build a farm here to feed my family, and a home, and I would become part of this island community.

Farmer Whetting His Sythe
William Sidney Mount, 1807-1868

Building the farm from cultural memory, I discovered Biodynamics and Rudolf

90

Steiner's call "to heal the earth" (H. Sehmsdorf, 2022, 203-217) through regenerative methods that minimized chemical and mechanical inputs. I embraced Aristotle's concept of economics as stewardship of the earth in imitation of nature. I was inspired by Thomas More's and Thomas Paine's ruminations on the "commons." Like Thomas More, I saw us not as owners of real estate but as "cultivators (of the land) who came in succession to live there" (H. Sehmsdorf, 2022, 218-222). I found fellowship and encouragement in the agrarian writings of Wendell Berry (1977), Gene Logsdon (1995), Fred Kirschenmann (2010), and many others. And I found my religious faith in the presence of the divine in nature confirmed in the theology of writers like Franciscan priest Richard Rohr (2019) and Episcopalian Ellen F. Davis (2009). The work on the farm became a religious task that helped me understand the Biblical quote I was assigned when confirmed

First building — Henning, Johann, 1976

in 1952: "It is a precious thing that the heart become firm, which happens through grace," *Hebrews* 13: 9 (*Es ist ein köstlich Ding, daß das Herz fest werde, welches geschiehet durch Gnade*).

Finding the land, however, proved harder than I had imagined. Where could I buy an affordable piece of ground close enough to Seattle? Traveling along I-5 during the summer of 1967, it became obvious to me that the corridor between Vancouver, Oregon and Vancouver, B.C. would soon develop into a continuous strip mall, with little room for an agricultural smallholding within driving distance of the city. Instead, I came to Lopez Island, and there found a suitable ten-acre property. Committed to the fundamental concept of no debt in developing the farm, I arranged for cash payments over three years. This required putting aside twenty-five per cent of my annual salary of $8,000, and in 1970 I took possession of the land. Three years later, my father offered an interest-free loan of $50,000 to build a house and dig a pond, in the form of a trust agreement that secured property rights for himself during his lifetime. We paid off the loan fifteen years later.

Building on the methods of Holistic Resource Management (Savory, 1988), I wrote a fifty-year farm plan to define our quality of life goals, forms of production and future resource base. Besides food production, farm programs would include education and community work, and we determined early on that at the end of our tenure on the farm, it would be gifted to the community through the local land trust. After my retirement from the University in 1994, we developed a Farm-to-School program (L.I.F.E.

Camp cooking, Sally, Käthe, Hexe, 1976

Garden, 2023) that brought local students to the farm three days each week. Wanting our animals to be butchered humanely, I proposed that the land trust develop a federally inspected mobile unit, the first of its kind in the U.S., now serving the San Juan Islands and near mainland (IGFC, 2023). We registered the farm as a non- profit organization under Washington State law, and in collaboration with local faith groups, developed a "Feed the Hungry program" (H. Sehmsdorf, 2016) to provide nutritionally whole, fresh food for people who could not afford to buy it in the market place. I joined Transition Lopez Island to help our island community become "fossil free by '33."

emphasis on human-scale economics and physical labor as an antidote to "nature deficiency" (Louv, 2008). Shortly before her death, however, my mother acknowledged that I had seasoned my "romantic" dreams with a dollop of "pragmatism." My father, on the other hand, loved the rural life and was a frequent visitor to the farm from the start.

Our beginnings on Lopez Island were pure Robinson Crusoe, living in a primitive shelter in the woods for several summers and on weekends throughout the year, while growing foods in a small garden and orchard. The kids loved sleeping in tents and hammocks, eating eggs from our own chickens, wild rabbits hunted on the place, and fish caught at the shore, bathing in water heated over the open fire, and generally running free in the forest and fields.

For a quarter century, we grew most of our vegetables and fruit in a quarter-acre garden. We also ran a cow and calf together with a neighbor's beef herd in exchange for his use of our pastures. We preserved the surplus of vegetables and fruit for the winter. Investing the money offered by my father, we built a cedar house, and dug a pond that vastly

Bathing in evening, Käthe, 1976

At first, my farm plans met with tacit opposition from University colleagues, who thought that I would "underperform" my professional commitments. I arranged for teaching schedules that allowed me to leave campus by Friday noon and return midmorning on Monday. I took repeated unpaid leaves. Neighbors in Seattle wondered why I preferred to work as an unpaid farmer during summers and vacations instead of going skiing, white-water rafting, or taking a road trip to Disneyland. Members of my family in Germany viewed the project with critical skepticism and a certain disdain for the holistic

Forest shelter, Käthe (on ladder), 1976

changed the ecology of our property by attracting countless birds, otters, frogs, newts, worms and spiders.

Elizabeth displaying CSA vegetables, 1990s

The scope of our farm activities changed radically when I left the University in 1994. While Elizabeth taught at the local high school, I concentrated on building farm infrastructure. For several years, we undertook a major project nearly every year, as incomes from farming and teaching allowed, always mindful of not going into debt. We increased the farm to fifty acres by purchasing neighboring properties, and by lease. We built two barns, a processing kitchen, a wood shop, a straw bale guest house, two greenhouses, and installed a water catchment and drip irrigation system, as well as solar panels to provide for the energy needs of the farm. We added beef and dairy cows, sheep, pigs, chickens, turkeys, and bees. We made hay, grew grain and baked bread, milked cows and made cheese. We sold vegetables to the community through a CSA. And we taught workshops, gave lectures, and wrote about our work.

In May 1997, all of my seven brothers and sisters came to celebrate my seventieth birthday, the first time we were all together since WWII, and also the last time. Two of them have died since then, and climate change is now making cross-Atlantic visits impossible. As we get old, what remains to be done is to hand the farm over to the next generation. We have settled two young families on the farm, exchanging equity in land and housing for labor. We are searching for someone to take on long-term responsibility for the farm as a whole.

The Immigrant Paradox — Trauma and Blessings

Community and Belonging

In 1967, Bob Dylan, self-styled folk singer following in the footsteps of Woody Guthrie and Leadbelly, sang a lament that I — an immigrant myself — have always found haunting:

> I pity the poor immigrant
> Who wishes he would've stayed home
> Who uses all his power to do evil
> But in the end is always left so alone
> That man who with his fingers cheats
> And who lies with every breath
> Who passionately hates his life
> And likewise, fears his death.
>
> I pity the poor immigrant
> Whose strength is spent in vain
> Whose heaven is like ironsides
> Whose tears are like rain
> And who eats but is not satisfied
> Who hears but does not see
> Who falls in love with wealth itself
> And turns his back on me.
>
> I pity the poor immigrant
> Who tramples through the mud
> Who fills his mouth with laughing
> But builds his town with blood
> Whose visions in the final end
> Must shatter like the glass
> I pity the poor immigrant
> When his gladness comes to pass.

When Robert Allen Zimmermann (Hebrew *Shabtai Zisl ben Avraham*) left the close-knit Jewish community of his family in small-town Minnesota, he changed his surname to Dylan — after Dylan Thomas, the Welsh poet — and became the "homeless" voice of his generation. Dylan's grandparents had arrived in the U.S. in the early 1900s: the maternal

grandparents from Lithuania, and the paternal from Ukraine, fleeing pogroms against the Jews. His forbears came from the small villages (*shtetls*) typical of Eastern Europe which had provided a strong sense of community based on the Jewish faith.

Just as other ethnic communities throughout Europe, the Jews of the *shtetl* (Little Town) felt rooted in the land. They shared a sacred history and a common language, and they lived in intergenerational families that included the dead. Much the same, other rural populations of pre-industrial Europe cherished beliefs in the "living dead." The dead would return to give advice or right old wrongs, and they were honored in solemn traditions on holy and popular feast days. The returning ancestors gave witness to the continuity of the family beyond death, and the living were securely implanted in the matrix of the traditional community. In Central and South America, the custom of visiting the dead on *Día de los Muertos* even now expresses the cultural link of family, faith, language, land, and work in shared community tradition.

Until their assimilation into the cultural mainstream, for most American immigrants from rural settings anywhere in the world, community meant the place-bound, trans-generational, rural populations that lived and worked close to the soil, and included both the living and the dead ancestors (Kvideland & Schmsdorf 1988, 83-125).

Until the middle of the 20th century, the majority of European immigrants to the U.S. came from such rural settlements and tightly knit village communities. The Jews from the *shtetls* of Poland, Russia, Galicia, Romania and Hungary were eternalized by Marc Chagall as the very symbol of Jewish identity in the diaspora. His iconic painting *I and the Village* —

one of many such pictures — expresses how deeply he mourned the loss of cultural ties of people and nature in the village community: the existential relationship of man and animal at eye level, the cow (or goat) as life giver, the relation of man and woman in work life, the fruit-bearing tree of life, and the embedding of the village community in the cosmic rhythms of sun and moon.

For the flood of Norwegian (and other Scandinavian) fishermen, loggers and farmers "the small community, the homestead, and the ancestral traditions in speech, food, and beliefs" became the image of their cultural home in the context of the new country (Lovoll, 1998, 3). For several generations, many Norwegian immigrants lived in closed communities in the new land, trying to retain their cultural identity, speaking their own language, practicing their faith and custom of contractual care of elder farmers passing on the land to the next generation within the community, a custom still common among the Amish today (H. Sehmsdorf 2020, 8f; H. Sehmsdorf, 2022, 220).

The permanent communities established by the Amish — religious emigrants from Germany and Switzerland in the 1700s and 1800s — still thrive today. One of their descendants, Dwight Eisenhower (formerly Eisenhauer), spoke Pennsylvania Dutch in his childhood and all his life ran the family farm in Gettysburg.

While most German, Irish, Polish, and Italian immigrants settled in urban areas, a significant number opted to establish agricultural communities, the Irish in the American South, Germans in Wisconsin, Poles in Minnesota, and Italians in California. Their communities were centered on their churches, and continued speaking native languages well into the 1970s. My children's Italian great-grandfather, for example, came to California where he became a so-called "lil' ole' wine maker" as part of the burgeoning industry mostly founded by immigrants from Italy.

Marc Chagall, I and the Village, 1911

One of our farm workers and his family immigrated after NAFTA (North American Free Trade Agreement) had robbed innumerable peasants in Central and South America of their economic bases. It is interesting to see that the Mexicans here on Lopez, while dispersed throughout the island, form a closely knit community sharing language, food and social traditions, and worship custom.

Until the middle of the nineteenth century, ninety percent of Americans still lived and worked in rural settings; by 1900 it was sixty percent; after WWI (and the end of federal subsidies for agriculture) thirty percent; by the middle of the twentieth century fifteen percent. After Nixon promulgated the fully industrialized mega-farm, the share of the population identifying as farmer reduced to one percent, and today the term "farmer" is not even listed in the census. The rest of the world followed the American example. The Soviet *Kolchóse* (collective farms) were organized on the American model. In 1989, after the Berlin Wall fell, I traveled to the island of Rügen in the Baltic Sea, hoping to see traditional farms in untouched landscapes. To my disappointment, I found that even in this remote outpost, agriculture had been industrialized: vast fields, here and there a super-sized tractor pulling an implement, no animals or farmsteads, hardly any people. Everywhere in Germany I found villages changed into bedroom "communities," interspersed with light industry, residual farmhouses turned into tourist accommodations, and the remaining fields combined in large-scale industrial enterprises.

Since 2021, fifty-six percent of the world population live in cities rather than in the countryside. These populations pay a high price for the demographic shift to urban hubs. Environmental psychologists posit that many city dwellers, and especially children, suffer from acute nature deficiency which radically changes the human brain and body (Louv, 2008). Personal health, community and closeness to nature go hand in hand. The world-wide civic organization Community Environment Legal Defense Fund (CELDF) aids remnant pre-urban — and aspiring "intentional" — communities (Foundation for Intentional Communities, 2023) in defending their legal right to the natural environments in which they choose to live.

Wild beekeeping, Black Sea, Turkey

The connection between personal health and community rooted in the natural environment is the subject of the acclaimed Turkish movie *Bal* (Honey). Shot in a remote eastern Black Sea region as the final installment of Semih Kaplanoğlu's autobiographical "Yusuf Trilogy" (2005-2010), the film explores Yusuf's early childhood in a traditional community of Moslem subsistence farmers who make their living raising wild honey bees and growing herbs for market. Some of the wild bees have disappeared, threatening the community's livelihood. The six-year old boy searches for his father, Yakub, killed in an accident while climbing a tree. The main characters are taciturn, and there is little dialogue. Instead, the soundtrack is filled with the muffled breathing of the forest and the cries of birds. It "makes you believe that you can smell the rain" (Nicodemus, 2010), and feel the wind and the sun on your skin (Tilmann, 2010). The villagers depend on the natural environment for their livelihood and on communal relationships for mutual support. The introverted boy develops a stutter in school, but an understanding teacher leads his fellow students in surrounding him with care. As the boy's mother falls into depression from missing Yakub, women neighbors comfort her, and the men mount a search for him in the forest. At an open air market on the village commons, slaughtered animal carcasses are sold and freshly prepared foods are eaten, and young and old share in ancient, lusty dances. But while the economy and lifestyle of

Yakub, Yusuf, and their hawk

the village bespeak a bygone era, certain images show that the community lives on the edge of the modern age. The hand-built wooden home is constructed from local timber, but it boasts a large modern refrigerator. At the open air market, meat cuts are packed in plastic shopping bags, and

Wild honey bees

the beekeeper's fashionable leather jacket comes from some distant city, as does the backpack the boy carries to school. This Turkish-German co-production reminds us that while some four million Turks (five percent of Turkey's population) live in Germany, many still identify with the culture of their homeland. When traveling in Germany in 2018, my wife and I found that many third-generation Turkish Germans spoke German with a Turkish accent and looked to their country of origin politically and culturally, rather than to the country where they were born. What they missed about urbanized Germany was precisely the natural environment and the village community their grandparents had left behind when they immigrated as "guest workers" (Mandel, 2008).

The fundamental problem for urbanized people is that by and large they no longer recognize their essential linkage to the natural environment. In spite of digital networks, city dwellers mostly live in isolation from each other. Community without access to nature degenerates into unmoored, self-centered individualism. The relentless drive for material gain undercuts the organic unity with nature that gives humanity its authentic place in the world. Today, the traditional term community has been replaced by virtual or digital "communities" of people who share certain interests: for instance, the Black community, the LGBTQ community, the Seahawks community, the Tesla community, or any other interest network. Google distinguishes so-called Brand Communities, Learning Communities, Social Communities, Network Communities, Fan Communities, World View Communities, and Local Communities. None of these "communities" involves a sense of belonging to the natural environment, of being rooted in a landscape, shared traditions of family, work, custom, religion or belief. Modern urban people live in self-imposed isolation, desperately searching for human belonging in virtual relationships and connections. Philosopher John Drummond coined the term "unified disunity" to distinguish the "thin"

understandings in virtual interactions in "dis-unified community," from the "thick" understandings of place-bound, trans-generational communities united by shared landscapes, history, faith, values, and economy (Drummond 2023, 1-17).

On this background, Bob Dylan's dirge about the "pitiful immigrant" can be read as a critique of American society and its materialistic values. His lament reflects the counterculture of the 1960s-1970s in rebellion against the dehumanizing socio-economic and political practices of the day. Dylan pities the immigrant who has to cheat and lie to survive, and "who falls in love with wealth itself, and turns his back on me," that is, on the tradition communities left behind.

Dylan's lament not only throws light on the cultural loss the singer likely felt himself, but is particularly relevant today in considering the deep cultural divides tearing contemporary America apart, for example, in response to the Covid epidemic. In May 2022, *The New York Times* compared death rates resulting from Covid infections in the U.S. versus Australia, Kenya and Norway. On a per capita basis, those three countries experienced death rates that were ninety per cent lower than those of the U.S. The primary reason for low Covid mortality seems to be a high level of trust between individuals, governments, and institutions in the countries to which America is compared, versus the starkly low levels of public trust in the U.S., where extreme individualism privileges personal choice over the common good.

Historically, the tension in immigrant experience between individual self-fulfillment and cultural loss is reflected in many immigrant narratives. A classic example is Ole Rölvaag's depiction of the Norwegian colonization of the Midwest (Rölvaag, 1932). Per Hansa is a natural pioneer who leads a group of immigrants in the large-scale exodus from Norway to America in mid-19th century. He comes from a small northern fishing

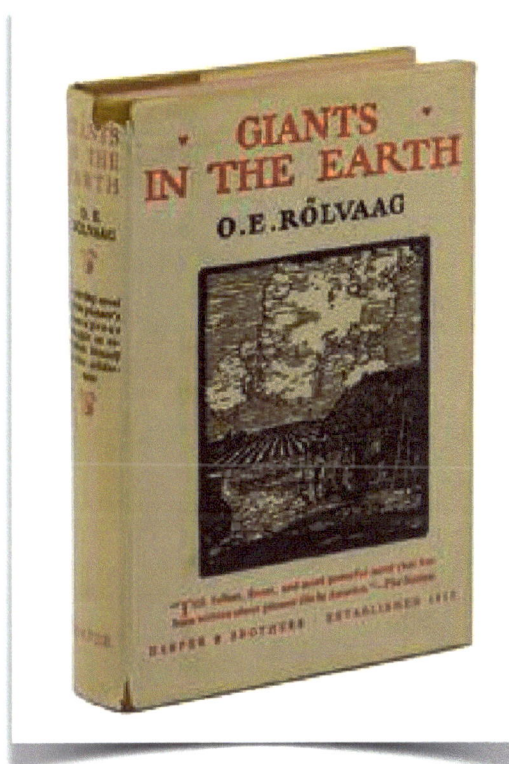

Rölvaag's immigrant narrative, 1932

community, where his master offered to buy him his own boat to assure him "a place at the top of his profession at the age of twenty, a chance to reign supreme in his little world," yet the young man turns him down. Why? The answer to this question is placed in the mouth of Rølvaag's tragic heroine, Beret, who grieves "the resistless flood that had torn them loose from their foundation and was carrying them helplessly along in its current...here on the trackless plains, (where) the thousand-year-old hunger of the poor after human happiness had been unloosed."

The cultural estrangement that drives Beret into madness comes from her deeply felt loss of family left behind in Nordland, from the loss of familiar landscapes of forest-clad mountains and sea, and the loss of traditional relationship to a natural environment she could understand and trust. Instead, she found herself thrust into a flat and featureless wilderness populated by strange animals and devilish Indians. The hundreds of thousands

of Norwegians settled in America by the end of the nineteenth century, stepped from the Old World in which nature was seen as alive and endowed with spirit, into a New World where nature was regarded as "demonic" by the religious, or as a resource to be "developed" by adventurous entrepreneurs (H. Sehmsdorf, 2020, 11f). Like Dylan's immigrant, Beret felt "always left so alone" in a world that filled her with dread:

"When the others had gone and the children were asleep, Beret rose and hung some heavy clothes up over the windows...to shut out the night. She felt that she could never go to bed, with all the eyes out there, staring in upon her. Last of all, she pulled the big chest in front of the door."

Robust individualism uncoupled from history and ties to traditional landscapes or beliefs, always has been and continues to be at the core of the American world view. No doubt, one of the causes of the socio-political divides in the U.S. today is that many see individual freedom under threat from environmentalists, and from government and corporate elites. For example, the filmmaker John Sayles in an "Ode to Simpler Days" (*Sunshine State*, 2002) bemoans the loss of the time when "a man (could) make his own way in the world... to carve a little something for himself... (that) went to the smartest, the strongest, the swiftest..., (and) if he couldn't survive the course, it was just tough titty." This tension between the loss of community felt deeply by the immigrant, and the individualistic self-assertion that dominates the American way of being in a commercialized world, can be tracked in countless films and art works.

The loss of community and the resultant loneliness experienced by immigrants in their adopted land was powerfully evoked in Andrew Wyeth's portraits of the Kuerner family, and in his famous *Helga Pictures* (1971-1985). These portraits consist of more than two hundred and forty paintings of Prussian immigrant Helga Testorf. She lived near the farm of the

Kuerner family, themselves immigrants from Germany who after WWI had settled in an early nineteenth-century farmhouse in Chadds Ford, a small township about twenty-five miles outside of Philadelphia. For more than seventy

Andrew Wyeth, *The German*, 1975

years, the Kuerner Farm was a major source of inspiration to Wyeth's depicting its people in hundreds of tempera paintings, watercolors and drawings with — in his own words — "pure, and deep, emotion." Wyeth portrays the earthy beauty of their ruddy, powerful faces and bodies, their passionate rootedness in the land, their love of work and austerity, order, discipline, and family cohesion. He also depicted echoes of the militarism the Kuerners had left behind in Germany in 1920. As art historian Brian O'Doherty wrote, "Wyeth's paintings of Karl and his environment often have a latent violence" (*Corn*, 1973, 24). Wyeth characterized Karl Kuerner as a hardboiled person, cruel and sentimental, with strong belief in the presence of spirit in the natural world. In the painting of the Kuerners and of Helga, the artist evokes the affinity of his subjects with "the bone structure of the landscape, the essential loneliness of it" (Wilmerding, 1987, 182). The images of Helga express love as well as tragic resignation, reserve and privacy. Interestingly, the painter himself identified with his putative Swiss-German background, a self-description his sister Carol questioned, saying that "What

Andy is depends on who he's painting." He once suggested that his painting of Karl Kuerner was a surrogate portrayal of his own father, whom he never painted. As an old woman, Helga Testorf said of her encounter with Andrew Wyeth, "I came to this country, and he found me. Everybody has a soul to share, and it's not so painful when you can share it…" (Testorf, 2020).

Andrew Wyeth, *Refuge* (Helga Testorf), 1985

The tragic murders on May 24, 2022 of nineteen children and two teachers in a Hispanic community in Texas throw light on the continuing immigrant experience — and the fraught sense of not belonging — in the context of the American culture of violence. The community of Uvalde, located in the Texas Hill Country, a few miles west of San Antonio and north of the Mexican border, has a population of fifteen thousand, of which nearly eighty percent are Spanish speaking. The hot, humid summers and mild, dry winters support an agricultural economy that produces vegetables, **animal feed**, honey, wool, and mohair, and freshwater fish. At Sacred Heart Catholic Church, services are held in Spanish. People live in multigenerational households, with grandparents and aunts and uncles and cousins. The beautiful hill-and-river country invites communal barbecues or floats down the Nueces and Leona rivers.

However, while most of the Latinos in Uvalde are employed as farm and service workers, the elites of the town are preponderately white. This is reflected in most socio-economic indicators: Average income in Uvalde is about forty-two percent lower than the average U.S. income, job growth twenty to thirty percent lower, and unemployment ten percent higher, resulting in a poverty rate of fifteen percent of the population. Employment in agriculture, fossil fuel extraction, and construction is up to ten times higher than the U.S. average, while professional employment is nearly seventy-five percent lower. High school, college and professional school graduation is close to fifty percent lower than the average in Texas. The city votes sixty percent Republican, forty percent Democratic, and all the "notable people" listed in the Wikipedia article on Uvalde, from a senator and U.S. vice-president to major sports figures, actors, gunslingers and notorious criminals, are Caucasians. The upside of these statistics is that workers in Uvalde spend half as much time commuting to their jobs, and while the city has only half as many physicians per capita, its water quality is twice as good as the U.S. average, and its air quality a quarter better, resulting in fifty percent fewer cases of respiratory diseases, and substantially lower rates of cancer.

The community response to the tragedy has been unified and heartfelt on individual, family, and institutional levels. The American Red Cross sent more than thirty volunteers to coordinate with local emergency officials providing mental and health services and spiritual care to families. Starbucks in San

Antonio sent workers because so many Starbucks employees had been affected. The American President and the Archbishop of San Antonio grieved with mourners in public, and Southern Baptists prayed on street corners. Family members brought food, bottled water, flowers and candles, wanting to be present and gathering in public places to offer small acts of kindness and comfort. Quiet conversations about gun control ranged from the reflexive Republican position that what is needed are "good guys with guns," to outrage that an eighteen-year old was able to purchase two assault rifles and

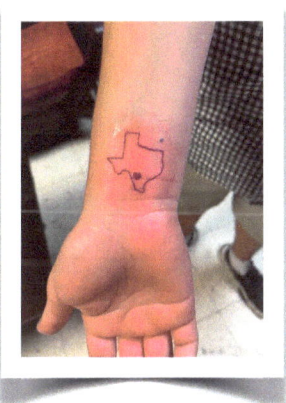

Community feeling tattooed on a youthful wrist in Uvalde, TX

nearly four hundred rounds of ammunition, and that the police delayed confronting the gunman, perhaps causing additional deaths. Texas senator Ted Cruz and former president Trump, speaking at the NRA national convention, made an unhelpful pitch to arm all school personnel and the general public, "a vision of society — if you can call it that — where every family is a fortress" (*New York Times*, May 28, 2022). The press corps packed parking lots in town with their rigs and equipment and knocked on doors for stories to report to the general public.

According to media reports, social workers, psychiatrists and violence and criminal justice experts hardly began to ask why a young man, barely an adult, would turn on his own family and neighbors. Why this shooting of mostly Latino children and teachers by one of their own? What disillusionment in the community of faith, ethnic bonds, family, and school drove him to pull the trigger? Was it a matter of personal pathology, or of a larger social rupture? What is the "unaddressed pain" behind his tragic behavior? How should the Latino community in Uvalde, and the public throughout the U.S., respond?

Eighteen-year old Salvador Rolando Ramos was bullied for his stutter and strong lisp. His mother, who lives with a sixty-year old man not her husband, is addicted to drugs, his father absent, and the boy was being raised by his sixty-year old grandmother, whom he shot during an argument. At school, he was skipping classes, getting into fistfights, cutting his face, and acting like a victim himself. In 2021, *Education Week* reported on an analysis of fifty-seven school shootings, finding that nearly half of the shooters reported a history of rejection at home and bullying in public (Sparks, 2021). But while bullying alone cannot explain mass shootings or predict violence, there is consensus that victims of physical, emotional or social abuse are more likely than non-victims to commit a violent crime.

Abuse, addiction, and poverty often enter into conversations about at-risk youth. In urban centers, especially in large cities, youths who feel disaffected from their own families and ethnic backgrounds, and from mainstream culture represented by church, school, and work, often turn to gangs. Most of the gangs, whether the historical English, Irish, German, or Polish gangs of the big cities on the East Coast, or the Asian, Black, White or Hispanic gangs of the West Coast today, were and are largely ethnically based. While in the past, gangs included both adolescents and adults who felt that their ethnicity stamped them "perpetual immigrants," today it is mostly youths responding to the stereotype as a racist or xenophobic form of nativism (Rathe, 2023). Racial minorities, as well as naturalized and even second and third generation native-born citizens are perceived as "foreign," because they belong to a minority ethnic group. In Uvalde, street and prison gangs consisting of predominantly Mexican Americans are pushing methamphetamine, cocaine, and heroin. But

there are no identified youth gangs in Uvalde, where a disaffected teenager could have found role models, a sense of belonging, friendship, status, self-esteem, and ethnic pride, however distasteful to the traditional Latino community. In a youth gang, "You've got brothers around, you're a family man" (Sondheim 1956/2021). Needless to say, gang membership in itself is not a panacea to the underlying problem of social isolation. On the contrary, it is a well-known fact that much of the systemic violence in American culture is perpetrated by gang youths, but the phenomenon of such gangs illuminates the loss of identity in populations who hold in common "perceptions of shared social experience or one's ancestors' experiences" (Peoples & Bailey 2012, 389). It seems clear that the Uvalde shooter felt cut off socially from his parents, school, church, and work, as well as from the traditional values of the Latino community embodied in the life of the grandmother, who took him in when his mother threw him out.

Psychiatrists hold that the kind of social trauma experienced by Salvador Rolando Ramos, can make it hard to process information quickly in a moment of threat — especially in the adolescent brain. When a teen also has access to a gun, readily made available through unregulated commercial channels, the result can be a pulled trigger before the consequences are considered. In this sense, the Uvalde murderer is another example of the "poor immigrant" who fills "his town with blood." A year later, *The New York Times* and *PBS News* reported on the anniversary of the tragic events in Uvalde. There were interviews and pictures of weeping parents mourning their dead children, expressions of outrage over the police department's failure to respond to the shooting quickly enough, and over the failure of the Texas Legislature to respond with meaningful gun legislation. President Biden took the occasion again to plead with Congress and the Senate to revisit the whole question of gun rights and public safety. Remarkably, however, there was no mention at all of the shooter and his family, of the immigrant grandmother he shot before he turned on his teachers and fellow students, or of the boy's drug-addicted mother, and his absent father. Nobody asked to what degree the cultural loss suffered by this second generation immigrant provoked the violent outburst that ended the life of so many in his community, including his own.

The question of how the shift in what community means in modern American society, and how this differs from the sense of community left behind by immigrants like myself, deeply affected my own sense of cultural belonging after I landed in the U.S. in 1956.

There is little doubt in my mind that my decision to grow the family's food on Lopez Island came from the immigrant's longing to make myself part of a cohesive rural community, strike root in the island soil in the tradition of my ancestors, and recover the deeply felt relationship to the sacred rhythms of nature. I earned the monetary means toward this end by teaching at a university, which meant that for too many years much of my time and energies were spent in the city. I remember the sense of dislocation while walking with my young family in the crowded, degraded city parks of Seattle, and the felt loss of meaningful interaction with the natural environment. But once on the island, surrounded by wild and farm animals, I felt at home in the silence of the place, where sun, wind, rain, heat, cold, and seasonal change shaped daily activities with much greater immediacy than in the city, and where the food we put in our mouths came directly from the work of our hands. I learned to love the island community, the mentors who taught me how to live on the land, the neighbors and friends the family relied on every day, the members of faith communities and social organizations committed to the common good.

My children grew up in two worlds and two opposing sensibilities: The island world where I felt connected to nature and community, and the urban world where I felt increasingly isolated from what mattered most. This dissonance increased in tandem with the growth of TV and social media and the artificial, virtual realities they propagated. The dramatic contrast between these irreconcilable sensibilities had large implications for our family life, and for our relationships with urban neighbors, colleagues, faith communities, and the social life of the city. While the contrast inescapably enlarged the cultural horizons of my children, it also burdened them with a divided sense of belonging. Did they belong in the community-based lifestyle, language, values, and behavior of an immigrant father who resisted assimilation to the American mainstream? Or did they belong in the world of cultural blandishments urged on them by playmates, city neighbors, schools, media, and commercial influence? While neighbors took their children to MacDonald's for "treats," we fed them homemade bread; while their children traveled with their families to Disneyland, we took ours to Lopez Island. Our children loved the untrammeled freedom of forest and fields, and of the island community, but they felt deprived when their city friends and schoolmates made them feel different for not having the same experiences. They felt that they did not belong.

The Immigrant Paradox

Many academic and public policies promote rapid immigrant assimilation. Yet, researchers have recently identified an emerging pattern, known as the "immigrant paradox." The paradox manifests on several levels.

The first level of paradox concerns an observation that many immigrants and their offspring over generations actually outperform native-born Americans in mental and physical health, educational achievement, and conduct, in spite of the social barriers many immigrants face in seeking acculturation (Vaughn 2014, 483-490). An example of the successful type of immigrant are the Pennsylvania Germans, as described by social historian Carl Wittke on the eve of WWII: "Like their Colonial ancestors, the Pennsylvania Germans of today are largely agricultural people, thrifty, sound, and substantial. Religion is still of the essence of their personality." The Mennonite background and life of Dwight Eisenhower provides a striking model of immigrant culture remaining effective over generations (Wittke, 1942, 85).

The inverse of the paradox concerns the observation that fully assimilated children of immigrants often experience diminished developmental and educational achievement in comparison to less assimilated immigrants over multiple generations. In other words, full acculturation potentially affects the children of immigrants negatively; the cultural loss experienced by the assimilated children of immigrants may impede their successful development. In a recent book-length study, psychologists, sociologists, educators and economists raised the question whether assimilation poses developmental risks. In comparing health, behavioral, and educational outcomes for foreign- and native-born children of immigrants across generations, they found that trans-generational biculturalism and bilingualism preserved immigrants' cultural strengths to the benefit of their offspring (Coll & Marks, 2011).

For most immigrants, mainstream communities are culturally unfamiliar at best, and often hostile or xenophobic. To mitigate mainstream hostility, immigrants have sought out ethnic enclaves that provide tangible social capital and relationships. Enclave networks promote exchanges of valuable resources and knowledge, lower language and cultural barriers, and offer economic opportunity and upward mobility. New immigrants tend to become employed by firms owned by immigrants of the same ethnic background who share their language and cultural world view (Waldinger 1993, 428-436).

As a Caucasian, I experienced less discrimination than migrants from other backgrounds, especially those who were less educated or less proficient in English. But having been born in Germany during World War II, for many years I was exposed to persistent ethnic prejudice when looking for employment, housing, and in many social contexts. Even today, in the eyes of many Americans a "German" is still regarded with cultural bias, in spite of Germany's having exorcised its Nazi past more thoroughly than, for example, America has its own racism and xenophobia.

My early employment experience in America exemplified the dual pattern of support by fellow German immigrants and mainstream prejudice. For instance, in Indiana my first job after immigrating in 1956 was offered by a German who had come to the U.S. in the 1920s and had become one of the biggest meat processors in the entire country. In fact, he made immigration to the U.S. possible for me. I met him in Germany at the firm where I was apprenticing in business. When he learned of my desire to pursue higher education — nearly impossible in post-war Germany — he used his influence to secure a Green Card within a few weeks and found work for me in one of his meat plants, which allowed me to attend community college in the evening.

On the other hand, in New York State, where in the early 1960s I looked for part time work to support myself while studying at the University of Rochester, I was repeatedly rebuffed by xenophobic employers, who would show me the door as soon as they found out where I was from. But I was hired by a German immigrant housepainter. He not only paid me a decent wage and accommodated my school schedule, but took me into his home, fed me with familiar foods and invited me on family outings. Even though I did not live in a defined German enclave, ethnic kinship with my employers provided both economic opportunity and cultural familiarity.

Both the meatpacker and the house painter

Dining room at Lüchow's, with famous painting "The Potato Pickers" by Swedish artist Auguste Hagborg

embodied a level of craftsmanship they had brought with them from their native country, where they had been certified as journeymen by

Freie Bibliothek und Lesehalle
(Free Library and Reading Room)

the German Chamber of Crafts (*Handwerkskammer*), just as I had. My employers hired me in the expectation that I would perform according to the traditional values and attitudes ("Prussian" virtues) they took pride in as markers of their own ethnic identity: Honesty, diligence, straightforwardness, conscientiousness, willingness to make sacrifices, orderliness, punctuality, cleanliness, frugality, determination, and reliability. These inherited cultural values served me well in

surviving harsh economic and social conditions in America. However, those same attitudes at times created tension in social situations for me, because they were perceived as rigid and judgmental.

Most scholars assess ethnic enclaves in terms of access to social programs, local markets, and employment opportunities. However, enclaves also offer relief from cultural and environmental estrangement. Ethnic enclaves tend to resemble the immigrant's place of origin in landscape or city architecture, the layout of homesteads or towns, language, values and shared beliefs. Besides the comfort of familiarity, enclaves provide relief from social hostility faced by immigrants in mainstream society.

The process of assimilation shapes how immigrants consider citizenship. I sought naturalization as early as possible to enable me to participate in the political process through elections. However, I never fully assimilated to the underlying American world view. The assassination of President Kennedy only a few days after I took the oath of loyalty to the Republic shocked me deeply. I felt dazed by the incomprehensible enormity of the murder of this young president who had so memorably challenged his countrymen to put country before self-interest, a sentiment that echoed my inherited sense of the commons (Simpson & Sehmsdorf 2019, 103). My despair deepened when shortly thereafter Robert Kennedy and Martin Luther King were also assassinated, echoing the feelings expressed in Bob Dylan's lament concerning the unfathomable culture of violence in the U.S.

Ethnic enclaves have been a constant in American immigration. The first enclave of English immigrants was chartered in Gravesend, Brooklyn in 1645 by Anabaptists excommunicated from Puritan settlements in Massachusetts. Most permanent enclaves were religious communities like the Amish, Hutterites, and other subgroups of Mennonites. The best-known urban enclaves formed with the arrival of large numbers of Irish immigrants during the first third of the nineteenth century, followed by successive waves of Poles, Jews, Italians, and other ethnicities during the twentieth century. As recently as 1998, nearly three quarters of all immigrants in the U.S. lived in city enclaves in California, New York, Texas, Florida, New Jersey or Illinois. By 1890, a majority of the German-born living in the United States were located in the "German triangle," whose three points were Cincinnati, Milwaukee, and St. Louis. According to the 2000 Census, the "most German town in America" was said to be New Ulm, some ninety miles southwest of the Twin Cities. Many of its residents still claim descent from German immigrants who settled there in the nineteenth century and stayed within the enclave. In the 1840s-1850s a huge German enclave, known as *Deutschländle* (Little Germany), grew up on the Lower East Side and East Village neighborhoods of Manhattan. By the middle of the century, eight hundred thousand Germans passed through New York City, which boasted the third largest German population of any city in the world after Berlin and Vienna. The immigrants clustering in this enclave tended to be educated and included master craftsmen, bakers, cabinet makers, masons and skilled construction workers. They established trade unions, breweries and beer gardens, gymnastics and shooting clubs, libraries, choirs, theaters, schools, churches, synagogues, political associations (*Vereine*), and New York's largest German-language newspaper, *Staats-Zeitung* (State News). The paper helped elect German American Charles Gunther as Democratic mayor of New York.

The city's most famous restaurant, Lüchow's, established by an immigrant from Hannover in 1882, introduced *Gemütlichkeit* (geniality; friendliness) into the heart of Manhattan (Haarskamp, 2022). It was said that through its doors passed all the famous people of the world, including Teddy Roosevelt, Padarewski, Mencken, Dvořák, Victor Herbert, Rogers &

Hammerstein, Fritz Kreisler, Theodore Dreiser, John P. Marquand, and a host of others (Simpson & Sehmsdorf, 2021, 141). Lüchow brewed his own beer. Prohibition came as a blow to him, but he never flouted the law. When it was finally repealed in 1933, New York's authorities honored Lüchow's with Liquor License Number One.

At its height, *Deutschländle* encompassed four hundred blocks of six avenues and nearly forty streets. The blocks were broken up into various neighborhoods of Swabians, Bavarians, Hessians, Westphalians, Hanoverians and Prussians, forming regional communities within the larger German enclave. From the end of the nineteenth century, just when second-generation German-Americans began to leave the increasingly crowded neighborhood to resettle in Brooklyn and other parts of New York City, Lüchow's survived as a valued monument of the past until it finally succumbed to urban blight in the 1980s.

The story of "Little Germany" in Manhattan illustrates the economic and cultural benefits provided to immigrants in ethnic enclaves. Enclaves enable immigrants to function successfully before adjusting culturally or linguistically to the host society (Portes & Jensen 1992, 418-420). By remaining segregated, immigrants can ease their entry into cultural norms and lessen the difficulty of assimilation. However, as a consequence of the war, by the time I immigrated in 1956, there

German emigrés leaving Hamburg for New York City
Harper's Weekly, 1874

studies required more and more of my energy, I opted for part-time work painting houses and fire escapes, selling hot dogs to summer vacationers at Lake Erie, working in a science lab, and as the chauffeur of an Anglican bishop. Once I qualified for scholarships to cover expenses at the university, I was able to stop supporting myself by manual labor. The biggest challenge during those early years as an immigrant was cultural isolation and a deep longing to put down roots. This I eventually satisfied when I found land in a small rural community and began to grow food for a family. The mental toughness instilled by my Prussian background helped me endure the long years of yearning for a home of my own.

It is instructive to review the arc of German immigration to the U.S. from the beginning of the Republic. Germans eventually comprised the largest ethnic group, exceeding even the English. The high mark of German immigration occurred in 1850s-1860s, with seventy percent of the total arriving by 1890. However, immigration from Germany had already begun during the Colonial Period, mostly Palatinate farmers who settled in religious communities in Pennsylvania and other states.

were no German enclaves left in the U.S. During and after the war, German-born citizens and their descendants hastened assimilation in order to protect themselves against the xenophobia gripping America. Thus they escaped the fate of a hundred twenty thousand Japanese Americans herded into concentration camps such as Manzanar in California. The sheer number of Germans in the general population, as well as the fact that as Caucasians they could not be identified as easily as Asians, insulated German Americans from this threat.

Like many of the immigrants in "Little Germany," I came to the U.S. with a modicum of professional qualifications. I had taken early graduation from a business school (*Kaufmännische Berufsschule)* and was certified a journeyman by the Chamber of Crafts. However, my ambition was not to work in business, but to seek higher education in the tradition of my family. My maternal grandfather had been a medical doctor, my paternal grandfather a philologist. My mother was an artist, and my father had written his doctoral dissertation on the legal authority of German consuls in foreign harbors. His hope to enter the German diplomatic service was cut short by the outbreak of the war. Upon first arrival in the U.S., I landed a blue-collar job in a meat factory, then used my business training to find employment with an importer of machinery from Germany. But as academic

Of the original Thirteen Colonies, only Pennsylvania had a truly bilingual culture, and many descendants of the Pennsylvania Dutch are still bilingual today, whereas most German Americans have lost their language, just like most other assimilated immigrants. But while holding tenaciously to their language and culture, as recently as in the 1940s, Pennsylvania Dutch were said to be "less Germanophilic" than the descendants of the English were Anglophilic, and had less connection with modern Germany than New England had with England (Wittke 1942, 1ff.) I felt this distinction deeply as a student of literature at the university. British and American poetry, for example, was seen as one continuous tradition, because it carried on that "quiet, pure stream of lyricism … that has its source in the early beginnings of English poetry" (Sanders et al 1968, XI). By contrast,

German and other European poetry was seen as foreign, not only in language but also in cultural substance.

By 1900, first and second-generation German Americans totaled nearly thirty-two percent of all Caucasian citizens in America. No doubt because of anti-German sentiments stirred by WWI, by 1930 the number of self-declared ethnic Germans had dropped to less than eighteen percent. By 1941, with the onset of America's involvement in WWII, the number of self-identified German Americans had dropped to a little over 1.2 million, a reduction of nearly eighty percent relative to 1930. Even so, by 2019, with an estimated number of approximately forty-three million, German Americans remain the largest self-reported ancestry group in the U.S., about one third of the total population of people of German ancestry in the world ("German Americans," 2023). Today, of course, most German Americans are fully assimilated into mainstream society and have lost their language and distinctive culture. However, some of the most iconic American foods such as apple pie, hamburgers, and hot dogs (*franks, wieners*), have German origins, as do other hallmarks of contemporary American culture. For example, Christmas trees or Santa Claus, the pot-bellied bringer of gifts invented by the Coca-Cola Company as part of an advertising campaign, build on Dutch and German traditions of austere Saint Nikolaus (Sehmsdorf, 2020).

Altogether, the story of German immigration to America is one of success, considering the criteria foregrounded by social scientists: economic security, health, and educational achievement. Once they left their ethnic enclaves, German Americans faced the same existential challenge as everybody else in post-modern, pluralistic society, which is the felt loss of community and belonging expressed in Bob Dylan's lament. Perhaps the singer chronicled what he felt when he left the tightly knit Yiddish community of his home town to become the troubadour of his generation. Until

fully assimilated, immigrants inescapably live in two worlds: old world traditions, customs and beliefs that emphasize community versus the modern emphasis on individual self-fulfillment and material success. To the degree that immigrants successfully negotiate the fundamental gap in opposing world views, their achievements often eclipse those of native-born Americans, as social psychologists have found. Many, however, fail, as the contemporary culture of violence amply demonstrates. The tragic story of the mass shooting in Uvalde, Texas, is a striking example of a second-generation immigrant responding in rage to a profound sense that he does not belong.

Researchers who investigated the "immigrant paradox" have tried to understand how second-generation immigrants are changed by the host culture (Coll & Marks, 2011). They found that while a bi-cultural upbringing offers significant value to the children of immigrants, it also poses substantial cultural burdens and challenges.

The involvement of parents in ethnic organizations and activities strongly influences their children's ethnic identity. Immigrants must promote their own cultural traditions if they want the second generation to identify with their ethnic backgrounds (Waters, 1994, 795-820). When my children were born in the 1970s, I tried hard to instill in them a sense of the German (Prussian) values and traditions I deemed central to my own identity. However, given the relative lack of a strong German presence in Seattle, I found little cultural resonance in the context of the city. There still exist six Protestant churches in Seattle originally established by German settlers between the 1880s and the first decade of the twentieth century. Some of them still offer occasional services in German, but otherwise the congregations have long since been assimilated to the surrounding culture.

The German Club (*Deutsches Haus*), the social center for Seattleites of German descent in the

1930s, today houses the German Heritage Society, which hosts occasional lectures, concerts and balls. A German-themed café named "Kafé Berlin" opened in the building in 2011, but closed again by 2016 for lack of patronage. The numerous German choruses, singing and gymnastic and other social clubs that thrived in Seattle prior to WWI, have given way to business-oriented organizations that bring together German expats and their descendants. For the most part they no longer speak German and mostly meet to cultivate business contacts.

German-style restaurants offer traditional beers and mass-produced, regrettably low-quality "Bavarian" sausages and other "traditional" foods. At the Oktoberfest in the faux-Bavarian tourist destination of Leavenworth, brass bands perform in ethnic leather pants (*Lederhosen),* but do not speak German or know anything about the culture. Similar commercial events are offered in Fremont, Kirkland, the Washington Fairgrounds in Puyallup, and on Queen Anne Hill, where beer and pretzels are served by pretty girls in fake Bavarian costumes (*Dirndls).*

Probably the most culturally alive German organization in Seattle today was — and still is — the German Language School, a non-profit organization that teaches German language and culture to children and adults on Saturday mornings.

Its curriculum includes traditional calendar events. On St. Martin's Day on November 11, the school organizes a children's lantern parade (*Laternenumzug)* with colorful self-made lanterns to light up the wintry dark streets, parks and forests. Saint Nicholas Day on December 6 (*Nikolausfeier)* is celebrated with traditional baked goods, warm drinks, and fire tong punch (*Feuerzangenbowle)* made by setting a rum-soaked sugarloaf on fire to drip into mulled wine. In February the school holds a carnival of exorcising winter (*Karneval),* with people in elaborate costumes dancing in the streets. In

Modern tourism poster

summer, the school organizes street parties (*Sommerfest),* open-air theatre and cinema nights under the open sky, and holds a seasonal book exchange (*Bücherflohmarkt).* My children attended the school only reluctantly because it meant giving up part of their weekends, while the neighbors' children were running free.

My faltering efforts to cultivate a bilingual German culture in my own family and home were complicated by the fact that professionally I had specialized in the study of Scandinavian language and literature, which pulled me into yet another cultural orbit. The Scandinavian House near the University of Washington campus offered traditional foods, music, dances and seasonal feasts. Troll Hill (*Trollhaugen)* ski hut at Snoqualmie Pass offered cross-country and down hill skiing and ski jumping. The Swedish Club in downtown Seattle, founded in 1892, hosted educational and cultural programs and celebrated traditional Swedish holidays. Seasonal events put on by the UW Scandinavian Department and in the homes of the faculty provided genuine cultural experiences mostly carried out in Danish, Norwegian, or Swedish, for which there was no equivalent in the German American community.

A further complication was that my wife, ethnically Italian, brought cultural traits to our family from her own background, such as an ebullient, emotional form of self-expression that contrasted sharply with my own cerebral and reserved Prussian style. My wife as an adolescent had been part of the 1960s hippie culture of Haight Ashbury in San Francisco, then the home to revolutionaries, famous singers such as the Grateful Dead and Janis Joplin, and radical social leaders, among them Herbert Marcuse — German-Jewish philosopher, who became the guru of the New Left, and Frithjof Capra — Austrian-born ecologist, and author of *The Tao of Physics,* 1975.

When my future wife came to Seattle, she sought to distance herself from the hippie culture and joined a Hindu religious community (*Vedanta*). This brought her into close contact with an ethnic enclave of Indians (many of them scientists working for the aircraft industry and Microsoft), and she adopted aspects of their social style, foods, and clothing. At the university, she was taking a degree in classical dance, to which she added study of German language and culture, which she came to love because it offered a cultural vision of the discipline she craved. She also felt that German philosophy and literature, especially of the Romantic period, provided a holistic view of individual freedom that meshed well with impulses from the hippie culture (Wulf, 2022).

My own response to that movement differed from hers. I was attracted to the revival of the Back-to-the-Land movement linked to the "Distributism" of the 1920s and 1930s which had attempted to find a "Third Way" between capitalism and socialism (Nuttgens, 2010). But I rejected the use of drugs and the sexual self-indulgence of the hippies (K. Sehmsdorf, 2005). In the 1960s, when a fellow student at the University of Rochester had offered me LSD, saying it would offer me ecstasy— I scoffed. Nature was the ultimate trip for me, and the idea of ingesting a chemical in order to experience ecstasy seemed perverse.

The poly-cultural amalgam of our family home created a challenging environment for our children, especially when they reached adolescence. The cultural expectations of each parent placed them between multiple world views, each embedded in its own ethnic background, which put them in conflict with the cultural conventions prevalent in our neighborhood and at school. From hindsight, it seems that we overlooked a cultural framework in which all these opposing impulses could have found a productive resolution: Waldorf Schools.

By and large, Waldorf schools in America no longer remember their origin in the social idealism of their founder, Rudolf Steiner. In 1919 Steiner established the first such school in Stuttgart, Germany at the Waldorf Cigarette Factory. His goal was to provide equitable access to quality education for the children of factory workers based on the concept of the human self enshrined in German Romantic philosophy. This philosophy was eventually brought to America in the writings of Coleridge, Thoreau and Emerson (Wulf, 2022). Fostering the creative power of the human self, self-reflection and self-awareness remain at the core of the Waldorf curriculum, cultivated through integrating the arts in all academic disciplines from preschool through twelfth grade. Music, dance and theater, writing, literature, legends and myths are not simply studied as curricular subjects, but experienced continuously in the long journey of personal development.

It is fair to say that American Waldorf schools today are elite institutions that sidestep the stated mission of public education, which is "to promote student achievement and *preparation for global competitiveness by fostering educational excellence and ensuring equal access*" (U.S. Department of Education). The idea of educational excellence fostered by Waldorf schools differs from that of the public schools. However, Waldorf schools no longer provide equal access for all students. While the first Waldorf School (*Freie Waldorfschule*) in Stuttgart was offered free of charge to the children of low-income workers, access to a Waldorf education in America today requires parental ability to afford steep tuition.

However, it is important to note that the elitism of Waldorf schools in America rests not so much on socio-economic class differences, as it does on cultural orientation. I remember my teenage children asking whether we were poor because we wouldn't buy certain things our neighbors took for granted. It was difficult for them to understand, let alone take pride in the fact that we distanced ourselves from the consumer culture. Our refusal to shop for the "best deals" in clothing, food, or entertainment exposed our children to sneers and bullying from their peers. In spite of my modest salary at the university, we would have scraped together the funds to pay for tuition if we had been aware of the educational opportunities offered by Waldorf schools. In fact, we eventually paid for the steep costs of sending the younger of our two children to a Catholic school in order to protect him from the violence common in public schools in Seattle, where students were bused from district to district in keeping with the government mandate of racial integration, "one of those well-intentioned social experiments that don't work," but undercut academic achievement and inhibited parental involvement (Tate, 2002). The older child, who was bused both in middle and high school, suffered academic and social damage from the busing. Sadly, while the Catholic school was socially safe, it did not offer a superior educational program.

While social equity is no longer at the core of Waldorf education, the curriculum provides students with pathways to develop intellectual, emotional, physical and spiritual capacities to become individuals certain of their own identity and ready for service to the world. Waldorf schooling emphasizes holistic advancement through creativity and imagination. The curriculum aims to inspire life-long learning in all students and to enable them to fully develop their unique capacities based on universal, timeless truths carried in

cultural and spiritual tradition. The idea that truth is inheritable and encoded in culture, has laid Waldorf schools open to the criticism that their curriculum is "mystical." However, the schools are not part of any church. Their curriculum espouses no particular religious doctrine, but is based on a belief that there is a spiritual dimension to human beings, to nature, and to all of life. The curriculum aims to build the students' capacity to internalize the knowledge that they are not merely material, social, and economic beings. As learning communities, Waldorf schools foster human relationships and promote the idea of social change through collaboration focussed on the common good.

From hindsight, it seems obvious that placing our children in a Waldorf school would have provided them with a different cultural environment from the public schools which inculcate conventional American values based on a competitive model. Most important, it would have given them a supportive peer group and reinforced the values offered to them by their own parents. Unfortunately, I did not know about Waldorf education at the time, and the very idea that parents had to compete for the best possible education for their children was foreign to me.

Trauma and Blessings

It is generally acknowledged that all human life is beset with trauma, beginning with birth. Birth trauma can refer to the experience of the mother, or that of the newborn. The mother's trauma can be physical, emotional or psychological, occasioned by what happens during labor and birth, or how the mother feels about it before or afterwards. The infant's trauma may result, for example, from in utero illness or from drug-induced labor, both of which occurred in my case. My mother suffered from gonorrhea while she carried me and was treated with quinine potentially harmful to the unborn, which is why my birth was hastened by repeated injections. It is also likely that the circumstances of her pregnancy and the birth saddled my mother with unresolved ambivalence that affected our relationship and had permanent effects on my physical and emotional health. Would I have become as introverted, and experienced the same degree of difficulties with social interactions, if my mother's pregnancy, my birth, and early childhood had been different? Would the bombings of Dresden in 1945 (when I was eight years old) have evoked the same terror if I had been more sure of my mother's protective love? Would I have experienced the same feelings of abandonment when circumstances after the war forced my parents to send me (and two of my brothers) to a boarding school when I was ten? Would I have felt as lonely and isolated after emigrating to the U.S. at age nineteen? Would I have failed in marriage to the mother of my children if I had been less self-absorbed and less uncertain of being worthy of love? Would I have been a better father if my sense of Prussian self-discipline had been less rigid and tempered by deeply experienced knowledge that in raising children the most important thing is love?

The blessings of self-awareness and release from trauma did not come easily to me. As C.G. Jung has postulated, waking up to self-knowledge comes from going within (Jung, 1973), but I found that I could not complete that journey until I was blessed with a wife who accepted me unconditionally in all my imperfections. Nor was the journey instantaneous or its goal certain. When I married again at age fifty to a woman fourteen years younger, it took years for me to trust the love offered by someone who had experienced unquestioning love both in childhood and in her first marriage (which ended in her husband's untimely death).

America offered me the blessing of choosing my own life path. After the loss of the family's ancestral home in Eastern Prussia (now an exclave of Russia), then the loss of the home of my childhood near Dresden, and the home of my youth at the boarding school for refugees in Hesse, I found new roots in the rural community of an island in the Pacific Northwest. Here I could plant my feet in the soil in the spirit of my family which goes back hundreds of years. Here I gained a sense of belonging to the degree that this is still possible in the twenty-first century.

Is belonging to place-bound community compatible with the modern emphasis on individual self-realization and diversity? America celebrates cultural diversity on the basis of the competitive market. People prize the freedom of mobility in pursuing economic and personal goals. The young are encouraged to leave behind limited educational or employment opportunities in small rural communities. The old are recruited by the tourist industry to shed community ties in favor of travel. Many commute between seasonal residences north and south. As a result, families are uprooted and generationally separated, the young and their elders living in different economic and cultural worlds defined by personal lifestyles. The very old end their days isolated in retirement communities and nursing homes. Belonging to community in the sense of place-bound shared economy, faith, and worldview, has been replaced by virtual communities of shared interests. The dead are mostly forgotten. Cremation replaces physical burial which requires care of the grave. At major holidays, like Christmas, separated families frantically criss-cross the country to reunite in brief visits fraught with unrelieved longing. People living together and taking care of each other is no longer an option for most.

Some of my German siblings occasionally questioned my choice to put down roots on a self-supporting, biodynamic farm. They saw it as a throwback to Nazi agrarian ideology that postulated the unity of defined populations with their settlement areas (*Blut und Boden* = "blood and soil"). However, in examining the inadvertent convergence of early alternative agricultural movements with the regressive agendas of the Third Reich, historians have discovered varying levels of support and rejection of biodynamics by Nazi authorities to suit their own political ends. Ultimately Rudolf Steiner's emphasis on the spiritual basis of holistic agriculture was anathema to Nazi ideology. Historians therefore have concluded that the history of "organic ideals of natural cultivation and regeneration, of healing the ravages of materialism and redeeming the land and its people" being coopted politically by the Nazis, must "not discredit organic initiatives as a whole" (Staudenmaier, 2013).

For me, choosing to grow my own food was not so much a lifestyle choice, as it was a spiritual necessity. Creating a committed relationship to the land became for me the foundation of community and belonging. It reminds me of Wendell Berry's poem "Stay Home" (1980). The writer extols the spiritual virtue of staying in place and submitting to the rigors of laboring in field and forest. As an immigrant, the freedom to pursue the biodynamic ideal without confrontation with political authorities, whether progressive or regressive, became the most profound blessing. As Steiner put it, " Every eternal idea that becomes a personal ideal, awakens life force in you" (Steiner, 2022, 28).

Another reproach sometimes levied against biodynamic farms is that they amount to attempted escapes into an imagined perfect world that never did and never will exist (*Heile Welt* = "wholesome world"). Steiner defined the task of the biodynamic farmer "to heal the world," by which he meant farming in a way that promotes the health of the farmer, the community, and the whole bioregion (H. Sehmsdorf, 2022, 206f). Wendell Berry has repeatedly pointed out what by now is obvious, that conventional economics, including agriculture, inexorably push us to climate collapse. A small farm allows for a sustainable alternative, providing health in the largest meaning of that term and inexhaustible lessons along the way (Berry, 2008).

Steiner knew this, as did economist E.F. Schumacher (1911-1977), author of the "eco-bible" that urges policy makers to adopt a global system "as if people mattered" (Schumacher, 1973). Detractors assert that the self-sufficient farm is no longer possible in a globalized world. Some neighbors scoff that a farm like ours cannot "make a living." We have found that while over fifty years our focus has been on "making a life" rather than "making a living," the farm has also succeeded economically (H. Sehmsdorf, op.cit., 23-34, 187-193, 211-217). My German family points out that owning such a farm in Germany would require the financial resources of a Bismarck and would be made impossible by regulatory restrictions governing farming. I count it a blessing that in America I have been able to pursue an academic career, while at the same time succeeding ecologically and economically on a small-farm scale. Berry reminds us that we live in self-imposed limits in society, and that our success or failure, our happiness and freedom, lie in voluntary self-restraint more than in economic barriers (Berry, op.cit).

Paradoxically, for me the key to surviving emigration and succeeding in my new home, were the vaunted Prussian virtues that can be summed up by the term Berry invoked: self-restraint. The cardinal virtues of mind and character in **classical philosophy** and **Christian theology** were prudence, justice, fortitude, and **temperance**. These formed the basis of the monastic vows taken by the Teutonic Knights when directed by the Pope to convert the pagan *Pruzzen*. The knights swore obedience to God and to the Master of the Order. In the early eighteenth century, these vows were raised to principles of state on which Prussia was built. The army and society were reorganized on the model of the Calvinist king as the embodiment of the Prussian virtues. Self-restraint to the point of self-denial, endurance without complaint, courage, and obedience tempered by frankness (*Freimut*) became core public and private values. Those virtues have a fraught history in recent German culture, and in my own family. The Prussian virtues introduced by the Calvinist king to bring order, discipline and fear of God into the affairs of state, were transformed by the Nazis into rigid standards of obedience and conformity to state authority (*Kadavergehorsam*). Frankness was no longer rewarded but incurred social repression and great personal risk.

However, until at least the end of WWII, the Prussian virtues continued to inform social expectations and the interpersonal dynamics of many, if not most, German families. In 1951, six years after the German capitulation, an aunt of mine wrote a story about a nobleman who gave up his life to safeguard his daughter from rape. In the following passage the daughter describes the role of the father, now dead, in her life:

"As Agnes prepared her father for the last journey, she took leave of him, and it seemed to her that she took leave of all refuge and belonging. The father had always been strict and his relationship to wife and children never intimate. Always, even at home in the circle of his family, he had been a Prussian officer, in whose book there were only three words: duty, honor, and fatherland. And he had taught them that their social rank, the nobility of an ancient and proud family, signified not privilege, but obligation. And so he had always remained remote from his own, but on the other hand he had also been the irrefutable, absolutely reliable norm of their thoughts and actions, a bulwark of certainty and calm. It now seemed to Agnes that he had left them behind in a rudderless boat in the middle of the wild ocean" (Marion Sehmsdorf, 2021, p. 12).

My parents were similarly remote from their children, and my father's favorite educational slogan was *noblesse oblige* (nobility obliges), mostly invoked to justify expectations of frugality, orderliness, punctuality, cleanliness, discipline, diligence, conscientiousness, toughness, endurance, willingness to make sacrifices, determination, reliability, and self-restraint .

The political and cultural re-education (*Umerziehung*) mandated by the U.S. military government after the War left deep wounds in the collective German psyche, as the country struggled to re-establish itself as a civilized nation. What had been conceived as virtues were now castigated as pride, arrogance, and cruelty. Germans today are loathe to invoke Prussian virtues as guides to personal and corporate behavior because they associate them with a history of submission to state authority during Nazi rule when self-confidence became arrogance, love of order petty pedantry, and fulfillment of duty abject inhumanity.

Broadly speaking, Germans on all social levels have been exemplary in examining the abhorrent Nazi record of dealing with ethnic minorities, Jews, Roma, the ill, homosexuals, or political dissidents. Culturally, the Germany of today is a much more egalitarian place than it was when I emigrated in 1956, eleven years after the end of the war. Since then the "miraculous" socio-economic reconstruction (*Wirtschaftswunder*) based on the idea of social justice in a market economy has taken root, a process more or less completed by the 1980s, making Germany once again the richest European country after WWII (Abelshauser 2005, 146-148).

Since the war, many political and socio-cultural leaders, among them Chancellor Helmut Schmidt (1974-1982), Matthias Platzeck, **President** of **Brandenburg** (2002-2013), and most recently Julius Schoeps, the Jewish director of the Moses-Mendelssohn-Center for European-Jewish Studies in Potsdam (1992-2014), have pleaded for a return to Prussian virtues such as politeness, punctuality, diligence, order, tolerance, and more, as fundamental civic values (Timm, 2012).

Schoeps points to Article 33 in the German Constitution which requires unselfish devotion to service, sobriety and objectivity in judgment, conscientious performance of duty, and absolute incorruptibility of every citizen. The Prussian virtues are thus part of the constitutional code, but they are mostly ignored in public discourse.

Recent government surveys of randomly selected populations and of more than a thousand elected officials showed that traditional virtues have lost ground in German culture. More than two thirds of respondents thought that values did not play any important role in politics (Geißler 2013).

The aim of the surveys was to compare the values of citizens with those of government officials and politicians, and throw light on the changing debate about values in Germany. Values were understood as either universal concepts — such as freedom — or as concepts based on personal experience. The study distinguished "primary" and "secondary" virtues — such as punctuality, diligence, or politeness — and asked which were particularly important for society, and how they might change in the future.

In contrast to political officials, more than fifty percent of the general population held that values were of little importance in public life. Only fifteen percent of the general population — but thirty percent of self-declared environmentalists — saw increased relevance of values in Germany's socio-political future. The majority ranked expediency, compromise, and pragmatism above values, and individual self-interest above the interests of the "commons." Religious faith and education of the "heart" were considered superfluous.

Nevertheless, among the values placed highest in German society today are the classical Prussian virtues of honesty, sincerity, candor and frankness, i.e. the willingness to express ideas and feelings candidly, a quality which in America is often regarded as tactless. Elected politicians ranked solidarity, justice, tolerance, and honesty highest, all values that also ranked high in historical Prussia.

According to the study, values are mostly inculcated by the social environment through direct communication, notably by parents and teachers for children, and for adolescents by friends and social media. Politicians, counselors, church representatives, celebrities have limited influence. People generally settle on their values early in life. Aware or not, by adulthood most people have a fixed set of values they follow.

In America, the question of values is equally fraught and fundamentally divides the country in right and left factions. As in Germany, American parents and schools seek to inculcate kindness, open-mindedness, tolerance, acceptance, and cooperation. But schools are also hotbeds of bullying, both the physical kind and in cyberspace. In the public sphere, dating sites call for partners who are kind and tolerant, but the marketplace is cutthroat and exploitive. Politicians claim values contradicted by their votes' serving self- and party interests. The American self-portrait in the television documentary "America: The Story of U.S.," celebrates competitive toughness as the central virtue that "makes America great" (Root, 2010). The American self-image is based on the idea of a level playing field and bootstrap individualism, both conditions rarely realized in the lives of average citizens.

Prussian virtues have helped me survive in the tough social environment of my new homeland, while I struggled to internalize the positive values of American culture. In my own experience, Prussian virtues are inextricably bound up with the German trauma of its political past — and therefore with personal trauma — but they have also been a blessing in the context of their intent, which is to serve the common good.

Seattle-based journalist Madeline Ostrander asks what it means to find a "home on an unruly planet" (Ostrander, 2022). Webster defines home as a person's native land, or the country of one's ancestors. By this definition, I would not be able to establish a home in the country to which I emigrated. However, the lexical meaning of home also includes one's dwelling place, abode of one's family and abiding place of affection, habitat shared by a social unit living together, or a refuge. These ancient meanings can be traced back to Holy Scripture. Hebrew בַּיִת (bayith) means shelter for animals or a family, and a place of return. In the Book of Ruth (1:21), for example, "bayith brought (Ruth) to return." In the New Testament, the Greek word ἐνδημέω (endēmēo) means to be at home. Its opposite, ἐκδημέω (ekdēmēo) means to be separated from home, or abroad.

Ostrander describes the wide-spread feelings of lost "connectedness to community and ecosystem and planet" as a kind of homesickness (Ostrander, 40). She traces the origin of the term back to Johannes Hofer, a physician who coined the term *Heimweh* (literally "home woe") to diagnose the mental pathology of survivors of the Thirty Years War (1618-1648) that devastated much of Germany. Hofer also invented the term "nostalgia" by combining the Greek words *νόσος* (nosos=return to the land) with *ἄλγος* (algos =suffering or grief), a term later rendered in English as homesickness (Anspach, 1934).

In German, *Heimweh* is linked to *Heimat* (homeland), a word that traditionally evoked feelings of safety and belonging to a particular place and connection with nature. But this term, too, is politically charged today, because the Nazis had exploited it ideologically.

In 2018, when the Federal Ministry of the Interior renamed itself *Heimatministerium* (Homeland Ministry), German journalists of color protested, because to them the term evoked a white majority society associated with racist, antisemitic, sexist, and heteronormative structures (Aydemir, 2019). Some of fourteen essays that comprise *Eure Heimat ist unser Albtraum* (Your Homeland Is Our Nightmare) seek to reclaim a more inclusive plurality in the term. Others reject its usage altogether because of its putative linkage with right wing violence in post-reunification Germany. As the American translators of the volume write in their introduction:

"The political discourse of the German *Heimat* has always been tied to the exclusionary and often violent history of German nationalism. It is rooted in the blood-and-soil fantasies of a conservative, white, Christian ethno-state, and the corresponding evocations of a timeless sedentism painted over the rural landscapes of German-speaking Europe. It offers a fantasy of homogeneity as anachronous in today's globalized world as it was in the multiethnic, multilingual territories of the pre-industrial Europe from which it emerged" (Cho-Polizzi & Sandberg 2020, 102-105).

Here the term sedentism, a technical concept which in cultural anthropology simply means the practice of groups living permanently in one place (Hirst, 2021), is used to pass negative judgement on Nazi ideologies of the past, and of putatively anachronistic fantasies said to be incompatible with the globalized world of the present. However, it can be argued to the contrary that sedentism— exemplified, for instance, by intentional communities in North America — constitutes a deliberate critique of the globalized world. Ecologists agree that globalization lies at the very root of planet-wide ecological destruction and climate change. Place-based rootedness and rebuilding the community of all living things — sedentism — may well provide the antidote to the despoilment wrought by globalization. Environmental philosopher Glenn Albrecht coined the syllogism *sumbiosity* to describe "a utopian-sounding state in which people lived in balance with the Earth" (Ostrander, 46):

"I argue that the next era in human history should be named the Symbiocene — from the Greek συμβίωση (sumbioson=companionship). The scientific meaning of the word symbiosis implies living together for mutual benefit, and I wish to use this profoundly important concept as the basis for what I hope will be the next period of earth history. As a core aspect of ecological thinking, symbiosis affirms the interconnectedness of life and all living things" (Albrecht, 2018, 2021, 2023).

German literary historian Friederike Eigler takes a balanced view of the term *Heimat* and its use in modern discourse. In a survey of how the expulsion of millions of ethnic Germans from Eastern Prussia, Silesia and Poland is fictionalized in postwar and contemporary novels, Eigler shows how German and Polish authors have responded to traumatic displacement in ways that unsettle the National Socialist politicization of *Heimat* without abandoning cherished, place-based notions of home (Eigler, 2014).

The German film Labyrinth of Lies (*Im Labyrinth des Schweigens*), based on the Frankfurt Auschwitz Trials (1963-1965) describes the beginning of the German reckoning with its Nazi past (Ricciarelli, 2014). A young and idealistic public prosecutor takes an interest in a former Auschwitz commander teaching at a public school in Frankfurt after the war. His efforts to bring the teacher to justice are initially frustrated because of former Nazis looking out for one another. Prosecutor-general **Fritz Bauer** (an assimilated Jew persecuted by the Nazis), puts the lawyer in charge of investigating former workers at the Auschwitz camp. The U.S. occupation forces give him access to their files, and he discovers there were 8,000 workers in the various extermination camps.

The historical trial was the first time a defeated nation ever tried its own citizens for crimes committed during a war. The film shows the moment when Germany's collective silence was shattered, forcing its people to own up to the nation's past. In spite of the widely publicized Nuremberg Trials (1945 – 1946) and the 1950 publication of Anne Frank's diary in German, as late as in 1958 one could ask a twenty-year-old in Frankfurt "What happened at Auschwitz?" and get a blank stare in response. The trials had great resonance within German society. A visitor to Germany today is struck by the ubiquity of Holocaust memorials in museums, churches, streets and public buildings. In 1993, German artist Gunter Deming (1947-) conceived of the project of installing stumbling blocks (*Stolpersteine)* on the sidewalks of cities not only in Germany and Austria, but throughout Europe where ever Nazis had persecuted Jews, Romani, homosexuals and the disabled. By one estimate, there are now more than one hundred thousand such engraved brass stones in front of former residences of Holocaust victims, a potent evocation of the link between the person's being and *Heimat*. The artist cites the Talmud saying that "a person is only forgotten when his or her name is forgotten" (Simonsen, 2019).

The history of the Holocaust is a staple of school curricula throughout Germany today. By contrast, I do not remember any mention of the Nazi past when I was in school in my home country. I remember rumors that our principal had been a war resistor and as a result was never promoted beyond the rank of private. I also remember that our physics teacher for years wore his jodhpur pants and high boots from his days as a WWII fighter pilot, but no one ever talked about his political role during the war. My Latin and sport teachers were austere and kind disciplinarians, but nobody thought about what their involvement with the Nazi regime might have been. My German and English teacher, who loved imitating Satchmo on his trumpet, must have been a soldier during the war, but this never came up.

We were taught nothing about the Holocaust in our history or any other classes. For the seven years I spent in the boarding school, the forest in which it lay, the fields, farms, and villages surrounding the school were *Heimat* to me, notwithstanding my longing for the lost home of my parents in Eastern Prussia and for the home of my childhood in the landscapes around Dresden. Our elders focused their attention and energies not on the war and Nazi ideology, but on the recovery of the defeated country. They used to say: "First there's the food wave, then the building wave, and then everything else (*Erst kommt die Fresswelle dann die Bauwelle und dann alles Andere).*

For many of us at the boarding school, the longing for home found expression in singing a lyric we thought of as a folk song, but actually was a German **Renaissance** song by **Heinrich Isaac** (ca. 1450–1517). The melody of "Innsbruck, I must leave thee" (*Innsbruck, ich muss dich lassen*) eventually became a Lutheran chorale and was used by Bach in several cantatas. We sang it often as a wistful lament that expressed our homesickness:

Innsbruck, ich muß dich lassen,
Ich fahr dahin mein Straßen
In fremde Land dahin.
Mein Freud ist mir genommen,
Die ich nit weiß bekommen,
Wo ich im Elend bin.
Usw.

(Innsbruck, I must leave you
I am traveling on my road
Into a foreign land.
My joy is taken from me,
and I won't be able to find it
When I am abroad in misery.
Etc.)

The analogy between a foreign place (*Ausland*) and being in misery (*Elend*, from Middle High German *ellende*, being banished from the homeland), was not lost on many of us at the school, who felt expelled from our birthplace, childhood home, or family.

I carried the longing for home with me to America, untrammeled by the political baggage ("culture wars") surrounding terms such as *Heimat* and the Prussian virtues, and their re-examination in German society after the Frankfurt Trials. Because I was a child during WWII, I had experienced the consequences of war: fear, hunger, rape, death, displacement. But I was not asked to take responsibility for the Holocaust the way my parents' generation, and even my siblings who stayed behind in Germany, were.

And so I was able to create a new home on a few acres where I could put down roots. In the 1970s, parallel with building an academic career at the university in Seattle, I found a place on Lopez Island, where my young family could breathe the fresh air, drink the clean water, and put our hands and feet into the living soil to grow food free of the toxins foisted on most Americans by the conventional food system. I knew that this new home would be a sacred place for me. In an interview by Bill Moyers celebrating the fiftieth anniversary of Wendell Berry's epochal book *The Unsettling of America* (1975), the author said: "There are no sacred and unsacred places; there are only sacred and desecrated places. My belief is that the world and our life in it are conditional gifts" (Moyers, 2014)

I held much the same values even before I knew of Berry's exemplary and inspiring work, and I incorporated them in a farm plan my wife and I have implemented over half a century.

For many years, I struggled with a sense of cultural separateness, but escaped the despair of the "poor immigrant" Bob Dylan evokes in his song, the madness of Rølvaag's tragic heroine, the aloneness of Wyeth's Kuehner and Helga, the helpless fury of the Uvalde's shooter, and countless others who responded to isolation with the culturally ingrained habit of violence.

Home — community — soil — roots — hope in difficult times. In one of his poems Wendell Berry says: "Hope then to belong to your place by your own knowledge of what it is that no other place is, and by your caring for it, as you care for no other place, this knowledge cannot be taken from you by power or by wealth" (Berry 2014). I found *Heimat* in this small place, this island community. And even though my ancestors rest in their graves far away from here, they are with me in this sacred abode. Blessings to All.

Lamb Slaughter

Soft muzzle resting
confidently in my hand,
you lean against my knee.

Memories of pulling you from
Your weakened mother,
Flasks of warm milk.

The sharp report from the gun
Drops you to your knees.

Swift cut of the knife severs
The artery in your throat,
My heart's blood seeps into the ground.

Lopez Island, 2023.

Sources:

Primary Sources:

Alver, Bente (1941-2020).
>1980-1985. *Brævveksling med Henning* (Correspondence with Henning). Unpublished.

Cherie. 1985. *Letter to Henning*. Seattle. Unpublished.

Dörbecker, Zimmermann, Koyro, Wagner (eds.) 1968. *20 Jahre Melanchthonschule: 1948–1958*. Steinatal.

Eisenberg, Hans-Helmut (1935-2020).
>1950-1954. *Steinatal*. Unpublished photo essay.

>1956-2021. *Briefe an Henning* (Letters to Henning). Unpublished.

Grude, Werner. (Great-grandson of Julius Sehmsdorf, first cousin of my father)
>1979. *Brief an Didi* (Letter to Didi/K.-E. Sehmsdorf). Unpublished.

Grude, Wilfried. (Great-grandson of Julius Sehmsdorf; first cousin of my father; my god-father)
>1981. *Brief an Didi* (Letter to Didi/K.-E. Sehmsdorf) Unpublished.

Kreis, Toni. (Granddaughter of Julius Sehmsdorf).
>1898. Photo of golden wedding anniversary, with identification of participants.

>1989. *Aufzeichnungen: Julius Sehmsdorf und seine Nachkommen* (Notes: Julius Sehmsdorf and His Descendants). Unpublished.

Köllner, Elisabeth. (Granddaughter of Julius Sehmsdorf).
>1924 *Familienchronik*. (Family memoir). Unpublished.

Müller, Frieda née Seyffarth. (Sister of grandfather Paul Seyffarth).
>N.d. *Die Sippen Seyffarth, Hesse, Starkowski, Schramm: Genealogie* (The Seyffarth, Hesse, Starkowski, and Schramm Clans: Genealogy). Leipzig.

Rautenhaus, Heike (1938-). (My sister; great-great granddaughter of Julius Sehmsdorf).
>2007. *Henning: Stationen eines Lebens* (Henning: Stations of a Life). Powerpoint.

Sedelmayer, Tim. (Second cousin; great-great-grandson of Julius Sehmsdorf).
>2018. Family genealogies, documents, photos. Unpublished.

Sehmsdorf, Elke (1941-). (My sister; great-great-granddaughter of Julius Sehmsdorf).
>1994. *Ein Sommer auf S&S Homestead Farm* (A Summer on S&S Homestead Farm). Unpublished photo essay.

>1999. *Wiedersehen!* (Return to Heidenau). Unpublished photo essay.

>2018. *Curriculum Vita*. Unpublished.

Sehmsdorf, Erich (1875-1940). (My grandfather; grandson of Julius Sehmsdorf).
>1894-1896. *Briefe an Meine Eltern und Schwester* (Letter to My Parents and Sister). Unpublished.

>1899. *Die Germanen in den Balkanländern bis zum Auftreten der Goten* (Germanic Settlements in the Balkans until the Appearance of the Goths). Leipzig.

>1907. "Zur Lehrplanfrage: Beiträge zur Gestaltung des Turnens an Höheren Schulen (Toward Curricular Development: The Role of Gymnastics at Secondary Schools," *Monatsschrift für das Turnwesen* (Monthly Journal for Gymnastics).

>1908. "Zur methodischen Schulung der Turnlehrer (Methodology of Training Gymnastics Teachers)," *Monatsschrift für das Turnwesen* (Monthly Journal for Gymnastics).

>1908. "Heyses *Kolberg* als Schullektüre" (Reading Paul Heyse's Historical Drama *Kolberg*, 1865, in Public Schools), *Zeitschrift für den deutschen Unterricht* (Journal for German Pedagogy).

>1909. *Program Realschule Kolmar in Posen* (Academic Program of the Secondary School in Kolmar, Posen). Kolmar.

1914. *Program Realschule Kolmar in Posen* (Academic Program of the Secondary School in Kolmar, Posen). Kolmar.

1914. *Das Schülerheim in Kolmar in Posen* (The Boarding School in Kolmar, Posen). Kolmar.

1931. *Stallupönen, Eydtkuhnen und Umgegend. Ein Illustrierter Führer* (Stallupönen, Eydtkuhnen and Environs: An Illustrated Guide). Stallupönen.

1931. "Das Stallupöner Bürgerbuch 1725-1819" (Citizen Book of Stallupönen, 1725-1819), *Archiv für Sippenforschung* (Archive for Family Research), 8: 13 ff.

1932/3. "Die Erhebung des Dorfes Stallupönen zur Stadt" (When the Village of Stallupönen Became a Town), *Mitteilungen des Vereins für die Geschichte von Ost- und Westpreußen* (Newsletter of the Historical Association of Eastern and Western Prussia), 7: 1-5.

1935. *Amtlich Beglaubigte Abschrift der Ehelichkeitserklärung von Julius Sehmsdorf, 1821* (Certified Copy of the Declaration of Legitimacy of Julius Sehmsdorf). Unpublished.

Sehmsdorf, Henning K. (1937—). (Great-great-grandson of Julius Sehmsdorf).

1937. *Das Buch der Kindheit* (Book of Childhood: Birth and Baptismal Certificates). Berlin.

1937-1962. *Heidenau, Steinatal, Rastatt, Rochester*. Photos.

1952. *Die Familie Sehmsdorf in der Westendstraße 4* (The Sehmsdorf Family on 4 Westend Street, Kassel. Unpublished booklet.

1952. *Konfirmationsschein* (Confirmation Certificate). Kassel.

1953. *Englandfahrt* (Trip to England). Unpublished diary.

1953-1954. *Deutsche Arbeiten, Melanchthonschule* (German Essays, Melanchthonschule). Unpublished.

1954. *Abgangszeugnis, Melanchthonschule* (Exit Grade Report, Melachthonschule). Steinatal.

1956. "Joseph Conrad's Heart of Darkness." Muncie, IN. Unpublished paper.

1957. *US Armed Forces Identification Card*. Washington, D.C.

1957-1961. *Papers and Diaries: Rochester, Frankfurt, Chicago*. Unpublished.

1955-2021. *Briefe an Hans-Helmut Eisenberg* (Letters to Hans-Helmut Eisenberg). Unpublished.

1958-1959. *Briefe an Eva* (Letters to Eva Schimmelpfeng). Unpublished.

1960. *B.S. Diploma*, U. of Rochester, NY.

1962-1979. *Correspondence with Winston Davis*. Unpublished.

1963. *Certificate of Naturalization*. Chicago.

1964. *Stilmittel & Stilprinzip: Studien zu Novalis' Heinrich von Ofterdingen* (Means and Principles of Style: Studies in Novalis's Heinrich von Ofterdingen). Chicago.

1964. *M.A. Diploma*, U. of Chicago, Ill.

1968. *Bjørnstjerne Bjørnson & Norwegian Folk Literature: Studies in Narrative Structure*. Chicago.

1968. *Ph.D. Diploma*, U. of Chicago, Ill.

1974. "Knut Hamsun's Pan: Myth & Symbol," *Edda*, vol. 6: 345-407.

1973-1974. *Käthe*. Unpublished photo essay.

1976. *Johann & Käthe, Vater's Visit, Lopez Island* (Johann & Kaethe, Father's Visit, Lopez Island), vol. I-II. Unpublished photo essay.

1980-1985. *Brevveksling med Bente* (Correspondence with Bente Alver). Unpublished.

1983. *Tagebuch der Ehescheidung* (Diary of A Divorce). Unpublished.

1987. *Wedding, Käthe & Johann* (Wedding, Johann & Kaethe). Unpublished photo essay.

1988. "The Dead and the Living," *Scandinavian Folk Belief and Legend*. Minneapolis, 83-125.

1990. *Auswanderung als Sozial-Kulturelles Problem* (Emigration as Socio-Cultural Problem). Göttingen). Unpublished lectures.

2003. *Trip to Germany*. Unpublished diary.

2005. *Agricultural Systems & Nutrition*. Unpublished notebook on Adam Drenowski Seminar, UW.

2016. *"Feed the Hungry:" A Collaborative Project of the Lopez Branch of the Lutheran Church in the San Juans, the Lopez Family Resource Center and S&S Homestead Farm.* Unpublished.

2020. *Myth and Tradition in Norwegian Literature and Folklife: Essays.* Lopez Island.

2020. *Continuity of Norwegian Tradition in the Pacific Northwest.* Lopez Island.

2020. "Nisse in Norway: From Farm Sprite to Bringer of Christmas Presents," *The Norwegian American* (Dec. 17).

2023. *Fifty Years of Biodynamic Farming: Essays.* Lopez Island.

2023. *Pentimento of Narcissus: Poem and Commentaries.* Lopez Island.

Sehmsdorf, Johann. (My son; great-great-great-grandson of Julius Sehmsdorf)
2016 1994-1995. *Briefe aus Arolsen* (Letters From Arolsen). Unpublished.

Sehmsdorf, Joachim (1913-1989). (Brother of my father; great-grandson of Julius Sehmsdorf).
N.d. *Brief an Werner* (Letter to cousin Werner Grude).

Sehmsdorf, Julius (1811-1900). (My great-great-grandfather)
1876. *Brief an August F. Pott* (Letter to August F. Pott). Unpublished.

Sehmsdorf, Käthe. (My daughter; great-great-great-granddaughter of Julius Sehmsdorf).
2005. "In the Wake of the Fifties: An Analysis of Two Parallel Movements in America." Unpublished paper (UW).

Sehmsdorf, Kurt-Eberhard (1905-1999). (My father; great-grandson of Julius Sehmsdorf)
1930's. *Familiengeschichte: Friedrich Sehmsdorf (1720-1809) und seine Nachkommen* (Family History: Friedrich Sehmsdorf (1720-1809) and His Descendants). Unpublished.
1932. *Die Polizeigewalt des deutschen Konsuls auf deutschen Schiffen in ausländischen Häfen* (The Police Authority of the German Consul on German Ships in Foreign Harbors). Göttingen.
1938. *Ischdaggen: Eberhard, Folker, Henning* (photo).
1940-1945. *Heidenau* (family photos).
1945. *Bad Harzburg: Henning, Elke, Kirsten* (photo).
1950s-1999. *Briefe an Henning* (Letters to Henning). Unpublished.
1980. *Brief an Klaus Ziemke* (Letter to Klaus Ziemke). Unpublished.
1991. *Göttingen: Elizabeth, Käthe, Johann, Henning* (photos).
1996a. *Interviews.* Bad Arolsen (Unpublished transscript).
1996b. *Notiz* (Notes regarding Julius Sehmsdorf and his children and grandchildren). Unpublished.
1996c. *Notiz* (Notes Regarding descendants of Ernst Sehmsdorf, oldest son of Julius). Unpublished.
N.d. *Stammbaum der Familie Sehmsdorf 1720-1930* (Sehmsdorf Family Tree 1720-1930). Unpublished.

Sehmsdorf, Lotte (1908-2003). (Sister of my father, great-granddaughter of Julius Sehmsdorf).
N.d. *Erinnerungen an meinen Vater* (Memoirs of My Father). Unpublished.

Sehmsdorf, Manfred (1953-). (My brother, great-great-grandson of Julius Sehmsdorf).
2020. *Versuch eines Stammbaums bis zu den direkten Nachkommen von Manfred Sehmsdorf* (Sketch of a Family Tree Including the Direct Descendants of Manfred Sehmsdorf). Unpublished.

Sehmsdorf, Marion (1906-2000). (Wife of Georg, oldest brother of Kurt-Eberhard Sehmsdorf).
2021. *Die Schöne Lilofee und dies und das aus dem Nachlass von Marion Sehmsdorf* (Beautiful Lilofee, and This and That From the Literary Estate of Marion Sehmsdorf, ed. by Eckhardt Sehmsdorf). Quedlinburg.
2021. *Zwischen Gestern und Morgen: Erzählungen* (Between Yesterday and Tomorrow: Stories, ed. by Eckhardt Sehmsdorf). Quedlinburg.

Sehmsdorf-Seyffarth, Ingeborg (1910-2000). (My mother, wife of Kurt-Eberhard Sehmsdorf, 1933–1948).

1929. *Gustav* (linoleum cut, with caption). Danzig.

1946. *Das Naschhafte Kathrinchen* (Greedy Little Kathrina, Illustrated Story). Unpublished.

1946. *Als sich der Weihnachtsmann verspätete: Eine Geschichte um Gernot's Lieblingsspielzeug* (When Santa Claus Was Late: A Story About Gernot's Favorite Toy). Unpublished. Illustrated in Pleasanton, CA and on Lopez Island, WA, 1985.

1946. *So pflanzt ich doch heute mein Apfelbäumchen* (And I'd Still Plant My Little Apple Tree Today). Wood cut. Heidenau.

1949-1950. *Münchhausen reitet auf der Kanonenkugel* (Münchhausen Riding on the Cannon Ball). Water color. Hannover.

1949-1950. *Münchhausen schießt das an der Kirchturmspitze angebundene Pferd herunter* (Münchhausen Shooting Down The Horse Tethered to Church Steeple). Water color). Hannover.

1974. *Sommer auf Lopez Island* (Summer on Lopez Island). Unpublished photo essay.

1974. *Vedanta Temple, Seattle* (Vedanta Temple, Seattle). Photos.

1974. *Seattle & Lopez Island*. Unpublished photo essay.

1976. *Reise nach Ostpreußen* (Journey to East Prussia). Unpublished travel description.

1980. *Weihnachten in Seattle*, vol. I-II (Christmas in Seattle). Unpublished photo essay.

Sedelmayer, Tim. (Second cousin, great-great-grandson of Julius Sehmsdorf)

2018. *Ahnenliste Henning Sehmsdorf: Einundzwanzig Generationen, 13.-20. Jhdt.* (Family Tree for Henning Sehmsdorf: Twenty-One Generations, 13th-20th Centuries). Unpublished.

Simpson, Elizabeth (1951-). (Wife of Henning Sehmsdorf, 1987—)

1991. "Seattle Punk," *Northwest Folklore*, 10 (1): 45-46.

Simpson, Elizabeth & Henning Sehmsdorf

2019. *Last Trip to Germany: Reflections on Art, Culture, Economics, History, Family and Travel in the Age of Climate Change*. Lopez Island.

2021. *Eating Locally and Seasonally: A Community Food Book For Lopez Island*. Lopez Island.

Uhrskov, Eva. 1981-1985. *Breve til Henning* (Letters to Henning). Unpublished.

Vesaas, Halldis Moren. 1981. *Brev til Henning* (Letter to Henning). Unpublished.

Walter (neé Sehmsdorf), Susanne (Daughter of Julius Sehmsdorf)

1935. *Brief an Käthe Grude* (Letter to Käthe Grude). Unpublished.

Secondary Sources:

Abbott, John S.C. 2017. *History of Frederick the Second, called the Great*. Scotts Valley, CA.

Adorno, T. W. 1857. *Noten zur Literatur I*. Frankfurt.

Albrecht, Glenn A. 2018. "Symbiocene Principles." https://glennaalbrecht.wordpress.com/2018/03/20/symbiocene-principles/. Retrieved June 4, 2023.

2021 Entering the Symbiocene. https://glennaalbrecht.wordpress.com/2021/11/10/entering-the-symbiocene/. Retrieved June 4, 2023.

2023. Applied Ethics in Human and Ecosystem Health: The Potential of Ethics and an Ethic of Potentiality. https://glennaalbrecht.wordpress.com/2023/06/01/applied-ethics-in-human-and-ecosystem-health-the-potential-of-ethics-and-an-ethic-of-potentiality/. Retrieved June 4, 2023.

Aldermann, Dirk 2000. "Hugo Lemcke als Reorganisator der Gesellschaft für pommerische Geschichte und Altertumskunde (Hugo Lemcke as Reorganizer of the Society of Pomeranian History and Antiquity)," *Baltische Studien: Pommerische Jahrbücher für Landesgeschichte*. vol. 86: 52-70.

Anspach, Carolyn K. (transl.) 1934. "Medical Dissertation on Nostalgia by Johannes Hofer, 1688," *Bulletin of the Institute of the History of Medicine*, vol. 2, no. 6: 376-391.

Arnim, Claus von (ed.) 2010. *Beiträge zur Geschichte eines uckermärkischen Dorfes im Landkreis Uecker-Randow* (Contributions to the History of an Uckermark Village). Carmzow-Wallmow, Germany.

Artikel 26: Grundgesetz für die Bundesrepublik Deutschland (Article 26: Constitution for the German Federal Republic). https://www.buzer.de/26_GG.htm. Retrieved June 10, 2012.

Atkinson, Emma W. (ed.) 1858. *Memoirs of Queens of Prussia*. London.

Aydemir, Fatma & H. Yaghoobifarah (eds.) 2019. *Eure Heimat ist unser Albtraum* (Your Home is Our Nightmare). Berlin.

Berghaus, Heinrich 1868. *Landbuch des Herzogtums Pommern und des Fürstentums Rügen: Schilderung der Zustände dieser Lande in der zweiten Hälfte des 19. Jahrhunderts* (Land Book for the Duchy of Pomerania and the Principality of Rügen: Description of the Conditions of These Regions in the Second Half of the 19th Century), part II, vol. III. Berlin.

Berry, Wendell 1977. *The Unsettling of America: Culture and Agriculture*. New York.
2008. "Faustian economics: Hell Hath No Limits," *Harper's Magazine*.
2010. "A Poem of Hope," *Leavings*, Berkeley, CA, 91.
2017. *A Small Porch: Sabbath Poems 2014 and 2015*. Seattle.
2021. "This Place That You Belong To." https://www.dailygood.org/story/2832/this-place-that-you-belong-to-wendell-berry/. Retrieved June 21, 2023.

Biewer, Ludwig 2000. "*Huge Lemcke, 1835-1925*,"*Baltische Studien: Pommersche Jahrbücher für Landesgeschichte*, vol. 86: 42-51.

Brooks, Christopher 2019. *Western Civilization: A Concise History*, chp. 8. https://human.libretexts.org/Bookshelves/History/World_History/Book%3A_Western_Civilization_-_A_Concise_History_I_(Brooks). Retrieved June 2, 2023.

Bundesamt für Justiz n.d. *Bürgerliches Gesetzbuch (BGB)* (German Civil Code). https://www.gesetze-im-internet.de/bgb/index.html. Retrieved June 10, 2023.

Capra, Frithjof 1975. *The Tao of Physics*. New York.
1983. *The Turning Point: Science, Society, and the Rising Culture*. New York.

Carlson, Michael 2008. "Earl Butz: US Politician Brought Down by Racist Remark," *Guardian*.

Carr, William 1979. *A History of Germany 1815–1945*. London.

Carsten, Francis L. 1989. *A History of the Prussian Junkers*. London & Berkeley, CA.

Černy, J. 1910/1920. (review) "*Kolberg*. Erläuterungen hierzu von E. Gülzow" (*Kolberg:* Commentaries by E. Gülzow), *Zeitschrift für die Österreichischen Gymnasien* (Journal For Secondary Schools in Austria), 376.

Cho-Polizzi, Jon & Michael Sandberg 2020. "Translators' Introduction," *Transit*, vol. 12, no. 2, 102-105.

Coll, Cynthia G. & Amy K. Marks (eds.) 2011. *The Immigrant Paradox in Children and Adolescents: Is Becoming American a Developmental Risk?* Washington, D.C.

Cord, Alix-Johanna 2007. "Bäuerliche Besitzverhältnisse in Gutsherrschaften" (Peasant Ownership On Estates), *Lübecker Beiträge zur Familien- und Wappenkunde* (Lübeck Contributions to Family and Heraldry Studies), 57: 7-13.

Corn, Wanda M. 1973. *The Art of Andrew Wyeth*. San Francisco.

Davis, Ellen F. 2014. *Scripture, Culture, and Agriculture: An Agrarian Reading of the Bible*. Cambridge, UK.

Davis, Winston 2001. *Taking Responsibility: Comparative Perspectives*. Charlottesville & London.

Deutsche Bundesbank 2023. "Purchasing power comparisons of historical amounts of money." https://www.bundesbank.de/en/statistics/economic-activity-and-prices/producer-and-consumer-prices/purchasing-power-comparisons-of-historical-amounts-of-money-795290.

Retrieved June15, 2023.

Drummond, John J. 2023. "Community: A Unified Disunity?" *Continental Philosophical Review*, 1-17.

Drygalla, Peter, n.d. *Das Verzeichnis der Leibeigenen im Amt Einfeld 1744* (List of Serfs in Einfeld, 1744). Family Search Catalog call number 943.512/E3 D2d.

    n.d. *Das Verzeichnis der Leibeigenen in den Ämtern Plön und Rethwisch 1744* (List of Serfs in Plön and Rethwisch 1744). Family Search Catalog call number 943.512 X2d.

Dylan, Bob. 1973. "I Pity the Poor Immigrant," *John Wesley Harding*. #BobDylan #IPitythePoorImmigrant #OfficialAudio. Retrieved June 1, 2023.

Eigler, Friederike 2014. *Heimat, Space, Narrative: Toward a Transnational Approach to Flight and Expulsion*. Rochester, NY.

Eliade, Mircea 2019. *The Myth of the Eternal Return: Cosmos and History*. Princeton.

Evans, Richard J. 1976."Prostitution, State and Society in Imperial Germany," *Past & Present*, vol. 70, 1: 106–129.

Feenberg, Andrew 1962. "A Course with Professor [René] Girard [The French Novel of the 19th and 20th Centuries]," Johns Hopkins U., http://www.imitatio.org/introduction. Retrieved June 3, 2023.

Flex, Walter 1917. *Der Wanderer zwischen beiden Welten* (Wanderer Between Two Worlds: An Experience of War). München.

Foundation for Intentional Community 2023. https://www.ic.org/. Retrieved June 10, 2023.

Friederich II of Prussia 1740. *Anti-Machiavel. Ou Essai de Critique Sur le Prince de Machiavel* (Anti-Machiavelli: Critical Essay on *The Prince* by Machiavelli). Edited by M. de Voltaire. Göttingen & London.

    1752. "Political Testament." In Macartney, C. A. (ed. & trans.) 1970. *The Habsburg and Hohenzollern Dynasties in the Seventeenth and Eighteenth Centuries*. New York.

    1767. *Memoires Pour Servir a l'Histoire de la Maison de Brandebourg* (Memoirs in Service of the House of Brandenburg. Berlin.

Fromm, Erich 1956. *The Art of Loving*. New York.

Frotscher, Werner & B. Pieroth 2005. *Verfassungsgeschichte* (Constitutional History). 5th ed. München.

Gerdes, H.-H. & H. M. Junghans (eds.) 2003. *Sören Kierkegaard. Gesammelte Werke und Tagebücher* (Collected Works and Diaries of Sören Kierkegaard), vol. 28. Simmerath, Germany.

German Americans 2023. https://en.wikipedia.org/wiki/German_Americans. Retrieved June 29, 2023.

Grass, Günther 1999. *Die Blechtrommel* (The Tin Drum). München.

Harskamp, Jaap 2022. "When Manhattan Spoke German: Lüchow's, Würzburger & Little Germany," *New York Almanack* (Nov. 2).

Hattenhauer, Hans (ed.) 1970. *Allgemeines Landrecht für die Preußischen Staaten von 1794* (General State Law for the Prussian States of 1794). Frankfurt & Berlin.

Haxthausen, August & Alexander Padberg 1839. *Die ländliche Verfassung in den Provinzen Ost- und Westpreußen* (Rural Constitution in the Provinces of East- and West-Prussia). Königsberg.

Henning, Friedrich-Wilhelm 1978. *Landwirtschaft und ländliche Gesellschaft in Deutschland, 1750 bis 1976* (Agriculture and Rural Society in Germany, 1750-1976), vol. II. Paderborn, Germany.

Herd, van Allen 2003. *The Concept of "Ungrund" in Jakob Boehme*. Norman, OK.

Herold, J. Christopher 2002. *The Age of Napoleon*. New York.

Heyse, Paul 2018. *Kolberg*. Whitefish, MT.

Hirst, K. Kris 2021. "Sedentism, Community-Building, Began 12,000 Years Ago," *ThoughtCo*, thoughtco.com/sedentism-ancient-process-building-community-172756. Retrieved June 1, 2023.

Hofferth, Sandra L. & Ui Jeong Moon 2016. "How Do They Do It? The Immigrant Paradox in the

Transition to Adulthood," *Social Science Research*, 57: 177-19.

Hollyday, F. B. M. 1970. *Bismarck: Great Lives Observed*. Hoboken, NJ.

Horn, James V. 2003. *Absolutism and the Eighteenth-Century Origins of Compulsory Schooling in Prussia and Austria*. Cambridge, UK.

Hölty, Ludwig C. H. "Der alte Landmann an seinen Sohn, 1776" (The Old Farmer to His Son, 1776). www.zeno.org. Retrieved June 10, 2023.

Island Grown Farmers' Coop (IGFC) 2023. https://www.nwlocalmeats.com/. Retrieved June 18, 2023.

"Immigrant Paradox in the United States." *Wikipedia*. https:// en.wikipedia.org/wiki/Immigrant_paradox_in_the_United_States. Retrieved February 1, 2023.

Jung, Carl G. 1973. *Letters, Vol. 1: 1906-1950*, Princeton.

Jung, Dirk 1982. *Vom Kleinbürgertum zur deutschen Mittelschicht. Analyse einer Sozialmentalität* (From Petty Bourgeoisie to the German Middle Class. Analysis of a Social Mentality). Saarbrücken, Germany.

Kane, Joe 1990. *Running the Amazon*. New York.

Kaplanoğlu, Semih 2005-2010. "Yusuf Trilogy," *Kaplan Productions*. Turkish film.

Kiepert, H. 1863. *Sieben Jahre Preussischer Verfassungsgeschichte, 1855-1862* (Seven Years of Prussian Constitutional History, 1855-1862). Berlin.

Kirschenmann, Frederick L. 2010. *Cultivating an Ecological Conscience: Essays From a Farmer Philosopher*. Lexington, KY.

Koselleck, Reinhart 1975. *Preußen zwischen Reform und Revolution: Allgemeines Landrecht, Verwaltung und soziale Bewegung von 1791 bis 1848* (Prussia Between Reform and Revolution: General State Law, Administration and Social Movement From 1791 to 1848). Stuttgart.

Krause, Tilman 2013. "Als die Jugend weg vom Rauchen und Saufen wollte," *Welt*. https:// www.welt.de/kultur/article120701441/Als-die-Jugend-weg-vom-Rauchen-und-Saufen-wollte.html. Retrieved, June 19, 2023.

Kučera, Rudolf 2012. *Staat, Adel und Elitenwandel. Die Adelsverleihungen in Schlesien und Böhmen 1806 – 1871 im Vergleich* (State, Nobility and Elite Change: A Comparison of Nobility Awards in Silesia and Bohemia 1806-1871). Göttingen.

Kürschner, Joseph (ed.) 2009. *Deutsche National-Literatur, historisch-kritische Ausgabe* (German National Literature: Historical-Critical Edition), II, 1: 287-315. Dearborn, MI.

L.I.F.E. Garden Program 2023. https://lopezislandsd.ss19.sharpschool.com/our_schools/ lopez_elementary/l_i_f_e_garden_program. Retrieved, June 18, 2023.

Logsdon, Gene 1995. *The Contrary Farmer*. White River Junction, VT.

Louv, Richard 2008. *Last Child in the Woods: Saving Our Children From Nature-Deficit Disorder*. Chapel Hill, NC.

Lovoll, Odd S. 1998. *The Promise Fulfilled: A Portrait of Norwegian Americans Today*. Minneapolis.

Mandel, Ruth. *Cosmopolitan Anxieties: Turkish Challenges to Citizenship and Belonging in Germany*. Durham, NC.

Mann, Thomas 1994. *Buddenbrooks: The Decline of a Family* (Buddenbrooks: Verfall Einer Familie, 1901). New York.

Marcuse, Herbert 1964. *One-Dimensional Man: Studies in the Ideology of Advanced Industrial Society*. London & New York.

McKeon, Richard 1941. *The Basic Works of Aristotle*. Chicago.

Merkel, Angela 2021. "[Expulsions of Germans after WWII:] An injustice." https://www.dw.com/ en/angela-merkel-opens-museum-on-germans-expelled-post-wwii/a-57982070. Retrieved June 10, 2023.

Mitford, Nancy 2019. *Life in a Cold Climate: Nancy Mitford; The Biography*. New York.

Moore, Steven 2013. *The Novel: An Alternative History, 1600-1800*. New York & London.

Moyers, Bill 2014 (interview). *Wendell Berry: Poet and Prophet*. Vimeo.com/76122933. Retrieved June 10, 2023.

Murdoch, Brian (transl.) 2016. *Walter Flex: The Wanderer between the Two Worlds: An Experience of War*. N.p.

Negus, Kenneth 1974. *Grimmelshausen*. Woodbridge, CT.

Nicodemus, Katja 2010. "Ein Festival aus Wahn und Schnee" (A Festival of Madness and Snow), *Die Zeit*, 2/10.

Nobel Prize in Literature 1910. NobelPrize.org. Nobel Prize Outreach AB 2023. <https://www.nobelprize.org/prizes/literature/1910/summary/. Retrieved June 9, 2023.

Nuttgens, Joseph 2010. "Letter," *London Review of Books* (May, 13).

Obenauf, Herbert 1984. *Anfänge des Parlamentarismus in Preußen* (Beginnings of Parliamentarism in Prussia). Düsseldorf.

Oesterle, Kurt 1998. "Die Heimliche Deutsche Hymne" (The Secret German Hymn). www.bdzv.de/preistraeger-preisverleihung/preisverleihung-weitere-jahre/preisverleihung-1998/kurt-oesterle/ Retrieved June 10, 2023.

Official Data 2023. "Value of $1 from 1800 to 2023." https://www.officialdata.org/us/inflation/1800? Retrieved June 1, 2023.

Onuf, Peter & Leonard Sadosky 2001. *Jeffersonian America*. Oxford.

Ostrander, Madeline 2022. *At Home on an Unruly Planet: Finding Refuge on a Changed Earth*. New York.

Peoples, James G. and Garrick Bailey 2012. "Humanity: An Introduction to Cultural Anthropology" *Sociology & Anthropology Faculty Books*, 9th ed. Belmont, CA.

Petersdorff, Hermann von (ed.) 1924-1935. *Bismarck: Die gesammelten Werke* (Bismarck: Collected Works), Berlin, 10: 139-40.

Portes, Alejandro, and Leif Jensen 1992. "Disproving the Enclave Hypothesis: Reply," *American Sociological Review*, vol. 57. no. 3: 418-420.

"Potsdam Agreement: Protocol of the Proceedings, 1945." In: Senate Committee on Foreign Relations & Department of State 1950. *A Decade of American Foreign Policy: Basic Documents, 1941-49*. Washington, D. C.

Rathe, Kaja J. 2023. "Forever Foreigners: The Temporality of Immigrant Indebtedness," *Journal of the British Society for Phenomenology*. https://doi.org/10.1080/00071773.2023.2205597. Retrieved June 7, 2023.

Ricciarelli, Giulio (director) 2014. *Labyrinth des Schweigens* (Labyrinth of Silence). German film.

Rogers, B.J. 1970. "Paul Fleming: Between Life and Dream," *Criticism*, vol. 12, no. 4: 259-270.

Rohr, Richard 2019. *The Universal Christ: How a Forgotten Reality Can Change Everything We See, Hope For, and Believe*. New York.

Rølvaag, Ole 1927. *Giants in the Earth*. New York.

Root, Jane (producer) 2010. "America: The Story of U.S.," *Nutopia*. London. Documentary.

Rougemont, Denis 1983. *Love in the Western World*. Princeton.

Sanders, DeWitt Gerald et al. 1968. *Chief Modern Poets of England and America*. New York.

Savory, Alan 1988. *Holisti Resource Management*. Washington, D. C.

Sayles, John 2002. "Ode to Simpler Days," *Sunshine State*. American film.

Scheel, Heinrich (ed.) 1966-1968. *Das Reformministerium Stein. Akten zur Verfassungs- und Verwaltungsgeschichte aus den Jahren 1807/08* (Stein's Reform Ministry: Records of the Constitutional History 1807-1808). Berlin.

Schiller, René 2003. *Vom Rittergut Zum Grossgrundbesitz: Ökonomische und Soziale Transformationsprozesse der Ländlichen Eliten in Brandenburg im 19. Jahrhundert* (From Noble Manor to Large Land

Ownership: Economic and Social Transformation of Rural Elites in Brandenburg during the 19th Century). Berlin.

Schmieder, Wolfgang 1950. *Das Musikalische Opfer* (Musical Offering), BWV 1079. Wiesbaden, Germany.

Schneider, Andrea 2013. "How Boys' Learning Styles Differ (and How We Can Support Them)." https://www.goodtherapy.org/blog/how-boys-learning-styles-differ-0211134#. Retrieved July 2, 2023.

Schumacher, E.F. 1973. *Small is Beautiful: Economics as if People Mattered.* New York. 1977. *A Guide for the Perplexed.* New York.

Scholar, Heather H. 1973. "Federal Farm Policies Hit," *Reading Eagle.*

Simonson, Michael 2019. "Stolpersteine—Commemoration and Controversy." Leo-Baeck Institute News 108. New York & Berlin.

Sondheim, Steven 1956. "Jet Song." https://www.westsidestory.com/jet-song. Retrieved June 1, 2023.

Sparks, Sarah 2021. "A Hallmark of School Shooters: Long History of Social Rejection," *Education Week*. https://www.edweek.org/leadership/a-hallmark-of-school-shooters-long-history-of-social-rejection/2021/09. Retrieved June 4, 2023.

Steiner, Rudolf 2022. *Wie erlangt man Erkenntnisse der höheren Welten?* (How to Gain Knowledge of Higher Worlds). 26th ed. Basel, Switzerland.

Storozynski, Alex 2009. *The Peasant Prince: Thaddeus Kosciuszko and the Age of Revolution.* New York.

Tate, Cassandra 2002. "Busing in Seattle: A Well-Intentioned Failure." https://www.historylink.org/file/3939. Retrieved June 9, 2003.

Testorf, Helga 2020. "I Was Andrew Wyeth's Secret Muse," *Muddy Colors: Art, Education, Community.* https://www.muddycolors.com/2020/01/i-was-andrew-wyeths-secret-muse/.

Tieck, Ludwig (ed.) 1821. *Kleist, Heinrich von: Prinz Friedrich von Homburg* (Prince Frederic of Homburg). Berlin.

Tillich, Paul 2015. *Ground of Being: Neglected Essays of Paul Tillich.* Aurora, Canada.

Tilmann, Christina 2010. "Das rote Band (The Red Banner)," *Der Tagesspiegel* (Daily Mirror), 2/17.

Timm, Ulrike 2012. "Historiker plädiert für Rückbesinnung auf alte Tugenden: Julius Schoeps im Gespräch mit Ulrike Timm" (Historian Pleads for Return to Old Virtues: Julius Schoeps in Conversation with Ulrike Timm), *Deutschlandfunk* (12/01/2012). https://www.deutschlandfunkkultur.de/historiker-plaediert-fucr-rueckbesinnung-auf-alte-tugenden-100.html. Retrieved June 21, 2023.

Trübner, Hans-Joachim 2011, "Zwischen Weltflucht und Weltsucht" (Between World Flight and World Addiction). file:///Users/maccomputer/Downloads perspektive_2011_07_zwischen_weltflucht_und_weltsucht.pdf. Retrieved June 13, 2023.

U.S. Department of Education. https://www2.ed.gov/about landing.jhtml#.~.text=ED's %20mission%20is%20to%20promote,offices%20from%20several%20federal%20agencies. Retrieved March 21, 2023.

Vaughn, Michael et al. 2014."Criminal Epidemiology and the Immigrant Paradox: Intergenerational Discontinuity in Violence and Antisocial Behavior Among Immigrants," *Journal of Criminal Justice* 42 (6): 483-490.

Waldinger, Roger 1993. "The Ethnic Enclave Debate Revisited,"*International Journal of Urban and Regional Research*, 17, no. 3: 428-436.

Waters, Mary C. 1994. "Ethnic and Racial Identities of Second-Generation Black Immigrants in New York City," *International Migration Review,* 28, no. 4: 795-820.

Weber, Max 2002. *The Protestant Ethic and the Spirit of Capitalism: and Other Writings.* London.

Wieck, Michael 1989. *Zeugnis von Untergang Königsbergs: Ein Geltungsjude berichtet* (Witness of the Fall of Königsberg: A Certified Jew Reports). Heidelberg.

Wilmerding, John 1987. *Andrew Wyeth: The Helga Pictures, 1971-1985*. New York.

Wittke, Carl 1942. "German Immigrants and Their Children," *The Annals of the American Academy of Political and Social Science*, vol. 223: 85–91.

Wolynn, Mark 2016. *It Didn't Start With You: How Inherited Family Trauma Shapes Who We are and How to End the Cycle*. New York.

Wright, Jerry 2001. "Christ, a Symbol of the Self," *C.G. Jung Society of Atlanta Quarterly News* (Fall), 6-8.

Wulf, Andrea 2022. *Magnificent Rebels: The First Romantics and the Invention of the Self*. New York.

Wuttke, Heinrich 1864. *Städtebuch des Landes Posen* (City Books of the District of Posen). Leipzig.

Zeuske, Michael 2019. *Handbuch Geschichte der Sklaverei. Eine Globalgeschichte von den Anfängen bis heute* (*Hand Book of the History of Slavery: A Gobal History From the Beginnings Until Today*). New York & Berlin.

Zuckmayer, Carl 1966. *Als wär's ein Stück von mir: Horen der Freundschaft.* (A Part of Myself: Portrait of an Epoch). New York.

Maps:

Old Prussia (https://en.wikipedia.org/wiki/Old_Prussians#/media/File:Old_prussians_12th_century.jpg).

*European Amber Road (*https://en.wikipedia.org/wiki/Amber_Road#/media/File:Amber_Road.jpg).

Extent of Teutonic Order, 1300 (https://en.wikipedia.org/wiki/Teutonic_Order#/media/File:Deutscher_Orden_in_Europa_1300.png).

Teutonic & Livonia Orders, 1422 (https://en.wikipedia.org/wiki/Teutonic_Order#/media/File:TeutonicOrder1422.png).

Brandenburg-Prussia, 1618. (https://en.wikipedia.org/wiki/Brandenburg-Prussia#/media/File:Locator_Brandenburg-Prussia_within_the_Holy_Roman_Empire_(1618).svg).

Brandenburg-Prussia, 1618-1648. (https://en.wikipedia.org/wiki/Brandenburg-Prussia#/media/File:Map_of_Brandenburg-Preussen.jpg).

30 Years' War (map-of-30-years-war-1.jpg).

Population Losses during 30 Years' War (population-loss-in-germany-during-the-thirty-years-war-l.jpg).

Confessions During 30 Years' War (range-confessions-result-Germany-Thirty-Years-War-1650.gif).

Holy Roman Empire, 1789 (https://en.wikipedia.org/wiki/Unification_of_Germany#/media/File:Map_of_the_Holy_Roman_Empire,_1789_en.png).

Prussia 1811 (http://www.antiqueprints.com/proddetail.php?prod=h1933).

German Confederation, 1811 (https://en.wikipedia.org/wiki/Unification_of_Germany#/media/File:Map-GermanConfederation.svg).

Prussia 1852 (https://www.mapseekerstore.com/maps-europe/maps-prussia-portfolio/old-map-prussia-1852-henry-george-collins-20347430.html).

Germany Unified by Prussia (https://www.britannica.com/place/Prussia).

Germany, 1871-1914 (https://www.zum.de/whkmla/region/germany/ksr7190dom.html).

German Empire, 1914 (https://nzhistory.govt.nz/media/photo/german-empire-1914).

East Prussia 1927 (https://www.pinterest.com/pin/384846730650672905/).

Counties in East Prussia (https://www.bildarchiv-ostpreussen.de/cgi-bin/bildarchiv/detailsuche/detailsuche.cgi).

Germany and Poland 1939 (https://www.pinterest.com/pin/3799980922584230/visual-search/?x=10&y=10&w=544&h=716&cropSource=6&imageSignature=665c80b22d6d2159a9ff32f0ec5992b3).

Territorial Losses, 1919-1945 (https://vividmaps.medium.com/territorial-evolution-of-germany-55fb78fea41a).

Königsberg (Russian *Kaliningrad)* (https://en.wikipedia.org/wiki/Kaliningrad).

Podanin, Poland (https://en.wikipedia.org/wiki/Podanin).

Stallupönen County (https://wiki-commons.genealogy.net/images/9/9d/Ebenrode_Landkreis.jpg).

Stallupönen (Russian *Nesterov)* (https://en.wikipedia.org/wiki/Nesterov).

*Wehlau (*Russian *Znamensk), Kaliningrad Oblast, Russia.* (https://en.wikipedia.org/wiki/Znamensk,_Kaliningrad_Oblast).

Züsedom, Mecklenburg-Vorpommern (https://mapcarta.com/17952992).

Germany Today. (858px-Map_Germany_Länder-de.svg.png).